The Sylvan High School Story

Ozzie's Boys

To Judy
Hope This book
brings back some
Golden Memories
Richard Hyatt

ISBN-10: 1466227443
EAN-13: 9781466227446

The Sylvan High School Story

Ozzie's Boys

by
Richard Hyatt

Table of Contents

Atlanta Constitution readers knew Cliff Baldowski as "Baldy."
His forte was political cartoons but in 1961 he illustrated the struggles
of Sylvan High's defending champions.

Introduction

This was one year out of our lives, only a moment really, but even half a century later it is a year that is washed in magic for those of us that lived in a tree-lined neighborhood on the south side of Atlanta.

Only what happened at Sylvan Hills High School in 1961 was not an illusion. It was real, very real, and the reality was played out during an enchanted basketball season that began with great expectations and ended with a scorebook of memories that refuse to fade.

Most of us never scored a basket or grabbed a rebound that year, but even then we sensed we were part of something important. We watched friends and classmates sweep through a year that was almost perfect. We came early and stayed late as the Golden Bears of Coach Ozzie Wadewitz roared through the regular season with relative ease, defying the so-called experts by winning their second straight state championship.

We savor the unbridled joy we witnessed on the faces of this gifted team as they celebrated victory after victory and we remember the pride we felt every day reading the headlines made by Lee DeFore, Tommy Roberts, Terry Stephens, Virlyn Gaynes, Bob Tuggle and their talented supporting cast.

We can still hear the thunder of cheering crowds that packed the house in Sylvan Hills. Many nights, we implored our team to score 100 points — an unheard of tally in that era. We cherish recollections of that electrifying night in 1961 when Georgia Tech's Alexander Memorial Coliseum was painted black and gold one last time. We wished 1961 would never end — and in many ways it hasn't.

Followers of that title-winning team have grown older, but their memories are surprisingly fresh as we look back at this special group and a season that gave a middle class school from the south side of Atlanta a temporary license to brag.

We are wiser now. We understand they were playing for more than themselves and more than their school. They were also playing for the anonymous residents of Sylvan Hills, Capitol View, Adair Park and neighborhoods in between — blue-collar folks that never went to school at Sylvan High. With every victory, these faceless people swelled with pride at the accomplishments and achievements of young men who lived down the street.

The individuals that made up that championship team more than 50 years ago are no longer young. The hop is gone from their jump shots and the fast break that struck fear in the hearts of opponents is not as fast it once was. They have families, careers and heartaches of their own. One member of that dynamic starting lineup — Virlyn Gaynes — died before reaching the age of 50.

Their old school has lost its identity. It is a middle school, which means the aging building still educates young people as it was meant to do. Because of its crumbling infrastructure, the schoolhouse often shows up on the city's demolition list though a special spirit still permeates through the building.

Sylvan High School graduates are scattered around the country, and so are members of that special basketball team. The players see each other once or twice a year for weekends of golf and storytelling. Like the rest of us, they only occasionally ride through an area of Atlanta that will always feel like home. When the 1961 basketball season is mentioned, the players replay every tick of the clock. Friends admire the love and respect they still carry for their old coach and the unspoken bond that morphs them into a team whenever they get together.

In them, the magic lives on.

———

Miss Ira Jarrell pushed for construction of a high school on Sylvan Road.

1

Where Sylvan Met Deckner

I t made its debut in 1949, so even old-timers hardly remember when the building wasn't there, perched on a hill overlooking the spot where Sylvan first met Deckner. From the beginning, it was more than just a schoolhouse where young people learned and matured. It was a place where dreams were made.

Generations of young people had for decades caught streetcars for bouncy treks across Atlanta's mid-section bound for Tech High, Boys High or Girls High. Bitter rivals when they competed, Tech High and Boys High shared a campus across from Piedmont Park that after World War II was transformed into Grady High. Girls High was in East Atlanta in a building that later evolved into Roosevelt High.

As the city recovered from World War II, a new philosophy of education was adopted and it was one not everybody applauded. It began to unfold in 1944, with the appointment of Miss Ira Jarrell as superintendent of schools. The former principal of Slaton Street Elementary School, she was best known as the activist leader of the local teacher's union. Jarrell was also the first woman ever to lead the Atlanta school system. She immediately pushed for change.

In an article she penned for *The Atlanta Journal Magazine* in 1945, Jarrell dared to criticize the deplorable conditions of the buildings at the city's beloved high schools:

> For a number of years, Atlanta's citizens have been embarrassed and mortified that her high school boys have been attending the last years of their public school career in portable, wooden structures — unsightly, unsanitary, unsafe. We have heard about our two junior high schools that were composed completely of portable structures ... It may well be to point out, too, that portable buildings are used not only for a senior high school, and a junior high school, but throughout the whole school system. Eight cafeterias, 12 auditoriums, and 10 gymnasiums are portable buildings. There are 116 classrooms which are entirely wooden portables, which means that one out of every 10 children enrolled in Atlanta's schools is housed in a wooden portable building ...

Jarrell decided that young people (and their families) would be better served if students went to high schools in their own neighborhoods. She also believed boys and girls would learn more readily if they went to school together. As part of her plan, junior highs were eliminated. Starting in 1947, students attended elementary school from kindergarten through the seventh grade and went to high school for five years. City leaders privately acknowledged the burden this would remove from Atlanta's decaying public transportation system — a system that for years had hauled boys and girls to and from school.

Showing surprising political clout, Jarrell successfully pushed for a bond referendum that brought in around $40 million for school construction — a hefty sum in that post-war era. Powerful alumni of Boys High and Tech High balked. They wanted nothing done that would jeopardize the status of their schools (and their athletic programs).

In 1947, the school board allocated funds for the creation of community high schools, including Grady, Bass, Murphy, Roosevelt, Brown, O'Keefe and Smith. Some were new construction. Some were converted junior highs. Left on the drawing board was a modern high school at 1461 Sylvan Road. Business

When Nabisco made Vanilla Wafers, the aroma fell on the community like a morning fog.

man E.J. Brewer helped the board secure property for a school at the corner of Arden Avenue and Sylvan Road, behind the busy Nabisco plant.

Other sides of town were not supportive, but Jarrell noted that southwest Atlanta was solidly behind the changes she proposed. Speaking specifically of West End and Sylvan Hills, she published this report on the status of public education in 1948:

> Atlanta communities are waking up. You might be amazed at some of the progress we have already made this year. The southwest section has really moved up on this new community idea faster than any other part of Atlanta. There in West End, community recreation centers are being developed not only at Joe Brown High School but at five or six of the elementary schools as well. Each of these is a place where children of all ages can play.
>
> The people of the community have been active, too. Members of the Southwest Community Council are co-operating beautifully with our staff at Brown … All over Atlanta our physical education program is branching out to include sports other than football and basketball so that we can reach more children. Some forms of recreation still cannot be developed in the community. Sid Scarborough, our athletic director, is

making arrangements for various schools to use the skating rinks and bowling alleys. This will be an after-school activity but a teacher will go with the children to act as coach. We already have swimming classes at the YMCA for students down to the sixth grade level. Atlanta as a whole must offer its youth more from a municipal standpoint ... We cannot overemphasize the fact that good communities will make Atlanta a better town.

The new community high schools have been more successful than anyone dreamed possible when they were organized last fall. They are also working all of us harder than ever before. Our teachers now have to go out and serve in the community as well as in he classrooms. Even the school buildings themselves are working overtime. We want these buildings to become community centers that are always open to any agency or group interested in boys and girls. The old buildings, designed primarily as classrooms, don't lend themselves too well to their new role. But as rapidly as possible we are bringing them up to date.

All of our new school buildings, like Murphy now under construction and Sylvan Hills to be built soon, will be designed to meet their new obligations to the community. Our new schools are planned so that certain rooms — libraries, auditoriums and gymnasiums — can be heated and lighted at night without opening up the rest of the building. Here the community can hold civic meetings and people of the neighborhood can take part in the educational activities of the school.

To the south, the airport was flexing its muscles. This was a place where families picnicked on Sunday afternoons while children and grownups alike marveled at the magnificent airliners that took off and landed. Now it was becoming a throbbing center of air travel for the region and a commercial hub that overnight set Atlanta apart from Birmingham, Chattanooga and Nashville.

Sports editors of the Journal and Constitution boldly suggested that the city would one day have a big league baseball team — unheard of in an era when National and American League franchises were clustered in the northeast. To shore up this farfetched proposal, writers said the city needed to build a big time stadium.

WSB-TV signed on in 1948. Owned by *The Atlanta Journal*, it was the city's first venture into a new-fangled technology that some believed would never catch on. Earl Mann, popular owner of the Atlanta Crackers, did not share this belief. He welcomed bulky TV cameras and scorching lights into Ponce de Leon Park and in 1950 fans watched games without leaving their living rooms.

Spectators fell in love with the daredevils on four wheels that stirred up dust at Lakewood Park. Their day job was running moonshine, but on Sundays they competed at the fairgrounds. NASCAR was founded in 1948, and local driver Red Byron won the organization's first sanctioned race and first seasonal championship. Fans cheered for drivers with wonderful nicknames like Cannonball Baker and Fireball Roberts.

Veterans came home from the war with visions of better lives for their families. A grateful nation provided the GI Bill, a package of benefits that helped them continue their education and finance new homes. Atlanta experienced a building boom after World War I, but growth following World War II was unprecedented.

Old became new, as historian Franklin Garrett described in 1954: "Between the end of World War II and the present time Atlanta has experienced a building boom, surpassing in residential construction volume (though probably not in quality) the great activity of the 1920s. Long familiar farmlands, pastures and vacant spaces throughout the area have sprouted row upon row of neat, comfortable, though for the most part, not distinguished, new homes."

Tethering themselves to the trackless trolleys on the No. 16 line that began circling the streets of Sylvan Hills and Capitol View (when drivers were not stopping to reattach the wires) and with the promise offered by that beautiful school on Sylvan Road, residents felt renewed.

Where there had been war, now there were dreams.

———

Sylvan's first graduating class dressed in formal wear instead of caps and gowns.

2
Hucksters in the Hills

Developers of Sylvan Hills sounded like hucksters offering suckers on a carnival midway the chance to see a woman with a flowing beard or a horse the size of a puppy as they described this subdivision being built near West End and Fort McPherson. When the hard sell softened, potential buyers discovered the beauty and value that those carnival barkers were selling.

The south side had begun to blossom in 1894 when the city limits of Atlanta extended into West End with the annexing of the old 7th Ward. An area around Oakland City that included Sylvan Road joined the city in 1910 with the annexing of the 10th Ward. In 1917, investors poured money into an area called Sylvan Hills — a fitting name, given the acres of trees and rolling hills.

Work on Capitol View, Adair Park and Westview was well under way when the development of Sylvan Hills began, using land that dated back to the Perkerson and Gilbert holdings from 1831. Numerous stories in *The Atlanta Constitution* offered reports so favorable that you wonder if the newspaper was among the investors.

Homes and lots were first offered for sale by the J.R. Smith & M.S. Rankin Company in the early 1920s. Articles ballyhooed the area's tree-lined beauty and accessibility to downtown. This story was published on May 13, 1923:

This splendid tract of gently rolling woodland is most appropriately named, because over its entire extent the gracefully undulating knolls are covered with majestic forest trees, shading the hills and vales during the summer season and furnishing much protection from winter blasts ... The many splendid building lots on this property have their own improvements, such as water, lights and other domestic conveniences ... The very reasonable prices asked for these beautiful lots and the liberal terms offered by the agency, make them highly attractive to home seekers. They are considered certain to advance in value as building continues and the population increases in this part of the city, which is looked upon as a thing certain to transpire. No part of Fulton County can show a more beautiful collection of building lots than are to be seen in Sylvan Hills.

A 1925 article quoted sales director O.L. Taylor:

Sylvan Hills is one of the show places of the south side metropolitan sections, giving ideal home sites for people who wish the residences just a comfortable distance from industrial centers. Another advantage is the accessibility to the city, the subdivision being located on Sylvan Road and reached by Dill Avenue and Lee Street, al of which are smoothly paved. The improvements are all down in the developed section, including Woodburne Drive, and the street improvements are being pushed to completion on both Harte Drive and Mickelberry Street. This is a delightful home center, and one of the most remarkable residential developments in this remarkable city. We offer more value, dollar for dollar, perhaps, than any other home subdivision in the south.

Sylvan Hills's development was built on the success of Adair Park, one of the city's earliest middle class neighborhoods. It was developed around 1892 by investors George Washington Adair, John Thrasher and Thomas Alexander It became a haven for homeowners attracted by its proximity to downtown. Adair was 22 years old when he started as a conductor on the Georgia Railroad. He accumulated enough money to help found *The Southern Confederacy*, a popular newspaper during the Civil War.

After the war, Adair started a local grocery business and ventured into real estate. From a terminal located in the West End settlement, he organized a fleet of mule-drawn streetcars that served all parts of the city. Realizing workers needed a way to get to work he developed residences close to public transportation — a concept used by developers today. Adair's fortunes mushroomed. His company eventually reported annual billings of $15 million. A red brick elementary school was built in 1912 near the beautifully manicured park.

CAPITOL VIEW MANOR also prospered. Prior to 1910, these neighborhoods on either side of Stewart Avenue were a pasture, owned by Andrew P. Stewart, Uncle John Shannon and the Deckner family. Streets were unpaved and no electricity or city sewerage was available. Life was so primitive that when the 12 charter members of Capitol View Baptist Church met in 1908, they walked by candlelight to their original building on Beatie Avenue.

Developer James Beatie used the area's excellent view of Georgia's capitol dome as a sales pitch but annexation and the arrival of public utilities in 1913 spurred most of the growth. Once it was annexed into the city, a number of original street names — duplicates of older Atlanta street names — were changed. Oak became Athens Avenue, Poplar became Belmont Avenue, Rock became DeSoto Avenue, Seminole became Allene Avenue, McPherson became Erin Avenue, and Elm became Beatie Avenue.

In 1954, Garrett noted how annexation contributed to Capitol View's growth. "Capitol View has continued to develop and has spread for a considerable distance east of Stewart Avenue. That part of the community was annexed to the city by degrees, partly in 1916, and partly in 1925 and 1926. The Capitol View Masonic Lodge, organized in 1914, built a three-story brick building on the northwest corner of Stewart and Dill avenues in 1921 from which a considerable shopping center has developed. The Capitol View Baptist Church, housed in a substantial edifice since 1927, now boasts a membership of well over 2,000."

Life prospered around the intersection of Sylvan Road and Dill Avenue and where Stewart Avenue crossed Dill — a road named for Charles Dill, a popular photographer and developer at the turn of the century. As the neighborhoods

Generations of Sylvan students hung out after school at Parramore's Pharmacy.

grew, residents needed places to do business. Filling the commercial needs of an army of loyal customers was a long list of neighborhood businesses.

- At the corner of Sylvan and Dill, Parramore's Drugs made tasty banana splits and filled prescriptions that were just what the doctor ordered. Roberts Drugs, in the Masonic building at Stewart and Dill, delivered items to your doorstep if you asked them to. These and other neighborhood drug stores provided after-school hangouts for youngsters on their way home from school.
- Owners of automobiles turned to Joe Mayfield or Cliff Jeffries when their vehicles needed their oil changed.
- Parents that wanted their children to learn how to play the piano took them to the homes of Mrs. Lawton Propes or Mrs. Chowning for lessons.
- People enjoyed eating out at Joe Cotton's or Pilgreen's. In the summer there were frequent trips to the Georgia Farmer's Market for white acre peas or fresh okra that mothers prepared just like their grandmothers taught them.

- People needing a florist to mark a special occasion called Mrs. Laney or Mrs. Chadwick for roses, wreaths or corsages — even at the last minute.
- Families pining for a sweet treat pulled their cars into the lot at Miss Georgia for a spinning wheel in a tall plastic glass.
- Neighbors needing a rake or shovel called Glenn Hulgan at Davis Hardware — next to the Sylvan Theater.
- Men thirsty for a quick bottle of beer on a hot afternoon sneaked into Brices's for a cold one.
- Mothers needing a loaf of bread or a can of soup sent their children to L.A. Welch and Son's Red Dot Store on Sylvan Road. The elder Welch was grumpy and not hospitable to young shoppers but until Colonial Stores and Kroger arrived, his store was a neighborhood fixture. Adair Park residents depended on Clarks's or Walker's and if they couldn't get there in person, boys on bicycles delivered items to their doorsteps.

Wartime shortages of building supplies curtailed construction but that changed with the availability of VA Loans. The announcement of a high school on Sylvan Road added to the explosion of home building in the area.

Built in 1928, Capitol View Elementary School still educates neighborhood children.

THE REST OF the city was concerned about other events. At the time, they seemed monumental. Generations later, some do not merit a second glance. They are reminders of how different 1950 Atlanta was from the metropolis of today.

At Ponce de Leon Ballpark, where ball players stole bases, Billy Graham prepared to save souls. Craftsmen went to work on a special pulpit and altar for the young evangelist's first Atlanta crusade as soon as the Crackers and boyish third baseman Eddie Mathews (a future member of the Baseball Hall of Fame) finished a pennant-winning season.

Lines of underground coaxial cable arrived from the northeast, promising more programming for WSB and WAGA, the city's TV stations. Kukla, Fran and Ollie came to town to mark the arrival of the cable but local kids were more interested in Woody Willow. They dreamed of celebrating birthdays on the marionette's daily TV show. (Imagine the excitement when Woody's creators, Don and Ruth Gilpin, later moved into Adair Park.)

Atlanta also took time to mourn. On August 16, 1949, a car hit Margaret Mitchell as she was crossing Peachtree Street. Five days later she died. A decade earlier, she had written *Gone With Wind*, the quintessential novel about the Civil War. It was required reading for Atlantans and the movie Hollywood made from it had its world premiere at the Lowe's Grand Theater. From that moment forward, Rhett Butler was Clark Gable and Scarlett O'Hara was Vivian Leigh.

On the north side, residents bitterly fought construction of a four-lane highway. That roadway meandered through town and eventually threatened the sanctity of Capitol View Manor. This was before people called it an Interstate. It was simply *The Expressway*.

An era in public transportation was also passing. On April 10, 1949, the city's last street car delivered its passengers. Reporter Dudley Brewer captured that historic moment in the *Atlanta Constitution*:

> Flat wheel and all, the last street car ran on Atlanta's streets early yesterday morning, and an era ended. It was in the small hours, when most streetcar riders are sound asleep, but there was a goodly crowd aboard with Operator John M. Harbin, oldest man on the River Line. It wasn't a crowd of revelers though. It was a rather quiet, reflective crowd, obviously

sentimental folks who thought it worth while to stay up all night just to ride a street car for the last time … There were people who have been riding street cars for years and now are riding the gleaming trackless trolleys — folks who make a city … Back downtown, as the last street car bumped up Broad and then Peachtree to Houston on its final weary way to the barn, the policeman on the corner turned to wave goodbye and the waitresses stood outside the all-night restaurant to watch 897 pass. At Butler Barn, all got out to watch them run her in on an empty track. An era spanning 78 years had indeed ended.

No one could imagine what the fate of those old streetcars would be. Their rusting carcasses were transformed into hot dog stands, hunting lodges or tourist cabins. Nor could anyone imagine what Sylvan High would mean to the people that lived around it. Landmark events were happening all over town, and for the people of Sylvan Hills, a landmark was being built before their very eyes.

It was a moment they would forever cherish.

———

D.W. Heidecker could hit an unruly student with an eraser from across the room.

3

The First Day of School

Eve was created from one of Adam's ribs and in 1950 — though old-timers from both camps may cringe at the analogy — Sylvan High was ripped from the very soul of Brown High, turning longstanding friends into neighborhood rivals.

"We wanted to be part of something new," explains Herb Britt, one of the students at Brown High School that opted to become a Golden Bear. He was part of something new but Britt and scores of others left behind the one of Atlanta's earliest settlements.

Before there was a West End or an Atlanta, there was a crossroads and a saloon called the White Hall Inn. Its name evolved from the fact that it had a coat of white paint while most houses in 1830's Georgia were left unpainted. From that crossroads at Lee and Gordon streets grew West End — a settlement connected to Atlanta by rail and roads.

In 1871, Richard Peters and George W. Adair bought out the Atlanta Street Railway Company. Mule-drawn trolleys soon made daily runs between a terminal in West End and Five Points, the symbolic center of the growing city. At the turn of the century, West End was alive with creativity and commerce.

Writers and journalists were among its residents, including Joel Chandler Harris, the creator of Uncle Remus. Other impressive homes belonged to city and state leaders such as Clark Howell, editor of the *Atlanta Journal*.

Joe Brown Junior High School — named for a former governor of Georgia — opened in 1923 at the corner of Peeples and Beecher streets. Built with a price tag of $280,000, it was designed to house 800 pupils in the seventh, eighth and ninth grades. Fifteen schools were built on land that cost $514,000 — an amount staunchly defended by Assistant Superintendent William A. Sutton.

"That doesn't strike me as being exorbitant," Sutton told a civic club. "The total cost of the land bought by the board of education, including fees for title, attorneys, etc., was $514,000, or about $4,000 an acre, and a large part of the acreage was in thickly settled sections. The 30 acres for the Boys High School site, near Piedmont Park, was bought for $75,000, or about $2,500 per acre. You go out and duplicate that for the money and I think we'll take it off your hands."

FOR MORE THAN two decades, Brown Junior High educated young people from Atlanta's south side. Its role changed in 1947 when high schools were created in every quadrant of the city. Officials also announced plans for a senior high in Sylvan Hills — just across the railroad tracks from Brown.

She was under fire, but Jarrell didn't flinch. "You can't exist without some controversy," she said. "People think different, and if you have the courage to do things you think are right, you are going to have disagreements."

As the opening of Sylvan grew closer, old allegiances were in jeopardy. Consider the household of Franklin Cullen Rodgers, Sr. Rodgers was a bona fide character. He never met a political office he wouldn't run for and his ability to make friends was legendary. His home was in shouting distance of Capitol View Elementary School and a short walk from the new high school. His oldest son — aptly nicknamed Pepper — was the quarterback of Brown High's 1949 state championship football team. His younger son, Allen, would attend Sylvan the following year.

In his lifetime, Pepper Rodgers played on a championship high school team at Brown and a national collegiate championship squad at Georgia Tech. He became a successful head football coach at the University of Kansas, UCLA and Georgia Tech and also coached in the United States Football League and Canadian Football League.

Pepper and Allen's father was caught in the middle. He had to choose between loyalty for Brown and hopeful feelings he was developing for Sylvan, where Allen was bidding for a spot on the football team. The elder Rodgers was a friend to both Rebel head coach J.E. DeVaughn and Sylvan's new mentor, Jimmy Green — Pepper's backfield coach at Brown. Rodgers got deeply involved in launching the new high school. He was the first president of the Sylvan High PTA and later represented the area on the city school board.

Such scenes were played out all over that part of town, for Sylvan's first student body was composed of young people that started high school at Brown. Connections continued when Sylvan's football team elected Charlie Ragan, a key reserve on Brown's championship team, as one of their co-captains. Ragan was president of Sylvan's first senior class and was voted the most athletic boy.

RELATIONSHIPS DID NOT end in the halls of the school or on the football field. Aware that the first principal of Sylvan would face unique challenges, Jarrell appointed D.W. "Ted" Heidecker to lead the new high school.

Heidecker came to Atlanta in 1923 for a job at the brand new Brown Junior High, becoming chairman of the school's Industrial Arts Department. A native of Minnesota, he graduated from the Stout Institute in Wisconsin. He received an undergraduate degree from Oglethorpe University and a Master's Degree from Peabody College. When Brown became a senior high school in 1947, he became an administrative assistant, preparing for the move to Sylvan three years later.

At Brown, Heidecker handled discipline — natural for a man of steadfast German heritage. Many male students assigned to Sylvan had experienced his wrath. They were also aware of his legendary throwing arm. "He could throw a blackboard eraser from across the room and hit his target right between the eyes — and usually his target was *ussuns*," laughs Herb Britt, a member of Sylvan's first student body, a letterman on its first football team and a member of the Class of 1952.

With so many students coming from an athletic powerhouse like Brown, officials recognized the importance of selecting the right football coach.

They turned to Green, a mannerly English teacher and a key component in building the city league's first state championship team. An article in May confirmed that Heidecker and citywide athletic director Sid Scarborough had hired the nucleus of Sylvan's staff. Scarborough, former coach of Tech High, announced Green as the Bears' first head football coach.

Joining him was Gene Golding, a lineman at Decatur Boys High and Erskine College. Scarborough tabbed Rod Colson as head baseball coach. The previous spring Colson had guided Bass High School to a city league baseball title. But the coup appeared to be basketball coach Paul Hoffman, a former star at Purdue University and the fledgling National Basketball Association.

Hoffman never taught or coached at Sylvan, however. Before school started, he decided to play another year in the NBA. Officials turned to Oswin "Ozzie" Wadewitz, a skinny minor league baseball player from Wisconsin. He played basketball at Milwaukee State Teachers College — now the University of Wisconsin-Milwaukee — and at Wheaton College in Illinois. His wife Rosemary was hired as a school secretary.

Atlanta schools braced for a tough year. A huge push in enrollment was forecast but officials assured the public it was prepared for the 10,000 new students. Assistant Superintendent J.I. Altman said systems all over Georgia faced increases. "It's because of three wonderful things," he said, citing an increase in the birth rate during the war, a growing tendency for students to stay in school until they graduated and new housing developments.

FOR SYLVAN, THE wait was almost over. Construction was done. Ceremonies were complete. A student body of 655 that had never met came together with a faculty and staff of 43 that had only recently met. They gathered in a building that still smelled new. While neighbors celebrated every brick and shingle added to the new schoolhouse, the principal assembled a faculty that would prove to be a strong foundation for years to come. Several came from Brown. Others were young teachers that would spend their careers at Sylvan. Included in that group was Gerald Culberson, an English teacher who 16 years later succeeded James C. Fain and become the school's third principal.

Members of that first staff and faculty were:

D.W. Heidecker, Principal; Mrs. C.R. Moss, Secretary; Mrs. Oswin Wadewitz, Secretary; Mrs. Mary Robertson, Nurse; Mrs. E.A. Broadwell, Cafeteria; W.C. Overton, Custodian and Mrs. J.C. Camp, Librarian

Sgt. George Adcock, Military; Elden D. Allian, Counselor; Miss Louise Bloodworth, Social Studies; Mrs. T.J. Bowers, Mathematics; J.C. Clegg, Science and Athletics; Mrs. William Collins, Science; Rodney C. Colson, Industrial Arts and Athletics; Wayne Cooper, Business Education; Gerald Culberson, English

Milton Earnest, Social Studies; Miss Rosa Fletcher, English; James B. Green Jr., Athletics and English; Robert A. Green, Mathematics; Miss Billie Green, Art; Carl Gunderson, Social Studies

Mrs. Donald Hayes, Homemaking; Miss Gail Hutchinson, Language; Mrs. B.L Jackson, English; Robert R. Jenkins, Music; Miss Joyce Lawler, Physical Education

Ted J. Mahoney, Industrial Arts; Mrs. Champion McAlpin, English and Mathematics; Miss Helen McGinty, Mathematics; Miss Martha Mills, Science; Sgt. O.J. Nunnery; Mrs. Henry P. Parrish, English

Grady L. Randolph Social Studies; Miss Ruth Rogers, Mathematics; Miss Frances Ryan, Homemaking; Miss Gene Smith, Music; Mrs. G.Y. Smith, Social Studies; L.E. Smith Jr., Social Studies; Miss Jewel Vandiver, Science; T.C. Vocalis, Business Education

Oswin Wadewitz, Physical Education and Athletics; James A. Wash Jr., Science; Miss Sara Dean West, Business Education' Mrs. Carl J. Wright, Business Education; Maj. Robert Wright, Military; and L.L. Young, Driver Clinic

Jimmy Green talks over his game plan with tackle Rausey Mason and halfback Jerry Williams. Mason was Sylvan High's first all-state football player. Williams, co-captain of the 1954 Golden Bears, was also a sprinter on the track team.

Teaching finally began — and so did football. Though the school was new, the Bears were founded on success since so many Sylvan players had experienced the joy of winning at Brown. Twelve athletes from Brown suited up but only Ragan had enjoyed significant playing time the year before. Several played on the 1949 city championship B-Team. Former Rebs that impressed Green in early drills were Ronald Miller, Stan Cochran, Emory Fears, Ed Carder, Charlie Epperson and Charlie Marmon.

No one thought preparing for a new school and a new football team would be easy but unexpected roadblocks developed. When practice began, locker rooms were unfinished and so were the showers. Dressing rooms were squeezed into a crude area near the boiler room in the bowels of the schoolhouse under the principal's office. A gym with permanent locker rooms would not be ready until 1954. That expansion would include a gym, nine classrooms, an auditorium and space for music and ROTC. It was dedicated May 9, 1954, bringing the cost of the Sylvan campus to $1.3 million.

Helmets were late in arriving but do not imagine today's high-tech headgear. These primitive head covers were leather and did not include facemasks. The practice field was nothing but heat and dust with a "Hill to Hell" that players dreaded. Goal posts were not erected until eight days before the opener. Practicing extra points or field goals was out of the question.

To make matters worse, assistant coach Gene Golding was called into the Army, leaving a gaping void in the coaching staff. Golding never made it back to Sylvan and a last-minute replacement had to be hired.

ON SEPTEMBER 14, 1950, the Sylvan High football team took to the field for the first time. Despite months of challenge and setback, the Bears defeated Spalding County, 7-0, at Memorial Stadium in Griffin, Ga. Halfback Stan Cochran scored the first points in school history and, with little practice, added the extra point. He set up that winning drive with a fourth quarter interception, grabbing an errant pass on Griffin's 20 and running it down to the 11. Charlie Corley gained five yards, setting up Cochran's scoring run from the six.

The most dramatic game of that rookie season came when the Bears and their old friends from Brown fought to a scoreless tie. Sylvan racked up the only score of the night — a pass from Ronald Miller to Troy Davis — only to have it erased by a holding penalty. That play was a microcosm of an up-and-down campaign that was marred by several key injuries. Sylvan finished its inaugural season 4-4-2.

Members of that first team are almost forgotten, but Green presented letters and jackets to the players in a December ceremony in the school cafeteria. Ragan, the team's co-captain, was the emcee.

Receiving varsity letters were:

Ed Carder, Billy Petty, Brewster Bailey, Bill Sutton, Bill Bingham, Gerald Adams, Tommy Crowe, Emory Fears, Charles Ragan, Charles Epperson, Charles Harmon, Frank Gossett, Jimmy Alley, Troy Davis, Allen Rodgers, Ronald

Brown, Rufus Chambers, Ronald Miller, George Chowning, George Cobb, Albert Price, Bill Stallworth, Ed Dortch, Jake Heaton, Richard Sandifer, Paul Woods, Gene Dyer, S.A. Poole, Charles Corley, Stan Cochran, Herbert Britt, Bill Moore (trainer) and Billy Orr (manager).

Green faced many obstacles but none greater than Wadewitz. Sylvan had no gym and no place to practice. Physical Education classes were held on an outdoor court at the rear of the school that wasn't suitable for a basketball team. When pre-season drills began, Wadewitz had to beg for gym time at Fulton High, Russell High or Brown High.

Despite the unusual challenges, the basketball team got off to a promising start, winning its city league opener against Bass High in early January. The Bears roared from behind and won 44-42 with a comeback sparked by Troy Davis with 13 points and Ronald Miller with 11. By the end of the month, the Bears had won five of their first six outings, trailing only unbeaten Brown. That set up a clash between the neighboring schools. The Rebels responded with a 58-31 thumping of Sylvan, sending the Bears into a late-season tailspin. Wadewitz's first team included Troy Davis, Ronald Miller, Charlie Ragan, Stan Cochran, Gene Bone, Allen Rodgers, George Cobb and Jimmy Hall.

Colson's baseball team had its moments but spring belonged to Jimmy Green's track team. They finished an impressive second to Lanier High of Macon in the state track meet. It was to be the best finish by a Sylvan track team in school history.

In the 100-Yard Dash, Emory Fears was first in the state with a dazzling 10.6 seconds. Fears also finished fourth in the Broad Jump. Richard Sandifer was third in the 100 and second in the 220. Ronald Miller was third in the 180-Yard Low Hurdles. The Half-Mile Relay Team of Fears, Sandifer, Charlie Ragan and Al Price took honors with a time of 1:33.5. That same group brought home medals in the Georgia All-Classification Meet.

LIFE WAS GOOD and so was school. There were challenges, however. Without a gym or auditorium, the only place students could gather was the cafeteria. Supplies arrived slowly but demands were met with a smile. The energetic faculty that Heidecker recruited quickly made learning something to celebrate. It was a year no one would forget.

Sylvan's Class of 1952 wore beautiful smiles and their Sunday best when they gathered for this class photo.

"We were true pioneers," Britt says.

At every turn, there was a first. Students elected class officers, planned school dances, organized clubs and organizations and created important traditions that were left in place for future students to enjoy. Students named and published the first school paper — *The Bear Facts* — and the first yearbook — *Golden Memories*.

Bobby Ward, a member of the Class of 1952, said faculty members cleverly let students believe these were their decisions to make. "Suggestions were planted in our heads by the teachers who made us think we had come up with the ideas. That was leadership."

123

Mistletoe Ball

SYLVAN HILLS HIGH SCHOOL

THURSDAY, DECEMBER 21st. 8:00 P. M.

SEMI-FORMAL

FREE REFRESHMENTS & DOOR PRIZES

$3.00 COUPLE OR STAG

Early students started traditions such as the Mistletoe Ball, an annual holiday dance.

The first issue of *The Bear Facts* included an open letter to members of the Atlanta School Board. Its title was *Dream Realized*:

> *We extend our deepest appreciation and thanks to the Board of Education for making it possible to build Sylvan High School. To most of the citizens of the Sylvan Hills community, it meant the realization of a dream they had long been holding in their hearts. Everyone watched with interest from the day the ground was first broken and the school slowly began to take shape. That interest was still growing as students began entering the building last fall, and it is going to continue growing, as year after year better-prepared citizens leave Sylvan to govern our world.*

In May 1951, the school's first graduation ceremony marked the end of the first year. Female graduates wore white dresses and males wore tuxedos. That was the style of dress for graduations until 1956 when seniors voted to wear caps and gowns. Student speakers were Joyce Lett, James Wesley and Sarah McGee. Seventy-three students were awarded diplomas:

Phyllis Dean Acree, Edward Brewster Bailey, Nancy Berry Beam, Joyce Blackstock, Barbara Jean Blackwell,

Richard Malcolm Bolen, Gerald Thomas Bone, Mary Jane Brisendine, Ronald Douglas Brown, Otis Spinks Bullock. Helen Louise Byrd.

George Chowning, Marie Wilhelmina Cochran, Lewis Reeves Cox, Jr., Norma Celestial Craven, Troy Austin Davis, Charles Cobb Deckner, Evelyn Ann Driver, Tommy Walker Drum, Nettie Elizabeth Dull.

Roger William East, George Herman Fauss, Jr., Joan Ruth Follett, Spencer David Fowler, Kenneth Leon French, Beverly Vaughn Gorman, Nancy Carolyn Gorman, Mary Jacqueline Grogan, Charles Ronald Harmon, Stella Harper.

Charles Julian Hawkins, Cleyson Jerry Haynes, Jacob Sanford Heaton, Doris Ann Hein, Frances Louise Heimly, William Conner Henderson, Patricia Ann Robertson Horton, Janet Johnson, Helen Marie Kelley, Mary Huff Kimberly.

Carol Lee King, Joyce Beverly Laney, Lois Jeannett Latham, Shirley Janeece Letson, Betty Joyce Lett, Margaret Gene Mayes, Martin Cameron McEntire, Sara Hope McGee, Donald Raymond Meaders, Ronald Lewis Miller.

James William Moore, Wilmer Regina Morris, Barbara Ann Ogletree, John Oliver, Jr., Clifford Monroe Payne, Dorothy Ann Perry, William Charles Petty, George William Price, Jr., Charles Edward Ragan, Janet Loree Ragsdale.

James Richard Sandifer, Bobbie June Snell, Thomas Aurelius Stallworth, Glenn Wood Summerlin Jr., Miclkeberry Franklin Thaxton Jr., Gail Jean Tilley, Helen Joyce Turnipseed, Rayann Elizabeth Wallace, Frances Kay Wellborn, James Wyatt Wesley Jr., Sara Catherine White, Shirley Jacquelyn Wyatt and Betty Louise Yancy.

No one wanted that historic year to end, but other excitement was echoing through nearby streets, inspired by the rhythm of hammers and saws. Construction was under way on residences on either side of Brewer Boulevard — a newly cut roadway that stretched from Deckner Avenue to Perkerson Elementary School.

New families were moving into the area. Enrollment at Sylvan Elementary School swelled requiring double sessions while workers completed five new classrooms. This would later translate into a spike in enrollment at the high school.

In the decades that followed, thousands of young people walked the halls of that new high school, but those 655 students that answered the roll in 1950 were the only ones that made the history books.

They were the original Golden Bears.

———

Billy Seabrook's family was the school's original next-door neighbors.

4

Eating Large on Sylvan Road

Apot-bellied stove heated the small garage apartment in back of 1487 Sylvan Road. Ben Seabrook, a finger print expert with the Atlanta Police Department, lived in the main house and out back he built the apartment for his son, Graham, and his growing family.

Graham Seabrook worked security at the Ford Plant near the airport in Hapeville. His oldest son, Billy, started to Sylvan Elementary School in 1948, but what the youngster really enjoyed were the hours he and other neighborhood boys spent playing in the heavy woods next to his house.

For a boy his age, taking a shortcut to "The Corner" through that dense urban forest was an adventure. There were no sidewalks on that side of Sylvan Road so Billy and his buddies were not alone when they took that well-worn path that emptied out on Arden Avenue. It was a popular walkway to Parramore's Pharmacy and the other stores at the corner of Sylvan and Dill.

Billy Seabrook was in kindergarten when he first heard noisy earthmovers crank up outside his window. Trees started to fall and so did the woods he knew so well. He couldn't understand what the commotion was about. To a small boy, those workmen were taking away his yard. He and his friends had run away from hornets in the thicket next to his house. Now they were told to stay away, that this was a construction site. At night, they disregarded those orders, sneaking on the property and dodging the night watchman that was supposed to be guarding the site.

"I remember after they had cut down hundreds of trees they piled up logs near the back of our house. Me and another boy that lived down on Deckner played in them, playing like they were forts. Climbing on those logs was dangerous, but we did it anyway. We were idiots," Seabrook recalls.

He was in the second grade when work was done and Sylvan High was complete. For most of their lives, he and his younger brother Larry were the school's next-door neighbors. His family eventually moved into the main house and when the gym was added in 1954, the campus was no more than 60 feet from their home. It was a great place to grow up, he says.

"I even learned to skate on that sidewalk in front of the school," he says. "I had never skated before but Mike Thurman was having a skate party for his birthday and I needed to know how to skate."

For Seabrook and for others growing up in that era, those neighborhoods might as well have been Mayberry for this was a place in which Andy and Barney would have felt at home. Sheriff Taylor could have gone home for lunch and a taste of Aunt Bee's award-winning pickles and Deputy Fife could have kept the peace with just one bullet. Mayberry is found only in reruns, but this area was real. It nurtured and protected young persons in ways it took them years to comprehend.

"OUR PERSONAL BELONGINGS were few, but the safety and comfort we felt with each other was our most valuable asset," says 1958 Sylvan graduate Pat Thomas Brannon, who grew up in the shade of the stately trees that guarded Adair Park.

Her idyllic memories of her neighborhood and that park are not very different from recollections shared by youngsters in Sylvan Hills, Capitol View or Perkerson. In the years between World War II and Vietnam, this area of Atlanta was untouched by the turmoil that came so quickly. Doors were left unlocked. Children roamed freely and safely. People looked out for each other and if you didn't score a touchdown or hit a home run today, there was always tomorrow.

Pat Thomas Brannon continues to be a cheerleader for her alma mater and for Adair Park. Before a late-season football game in 1957, she and Jane Voss helped decorate the team bus.

Its environment was wrapped in an innocence that soon faded and disappeared. Alcohol was not a serious issue, though someone could always whisper the number of a carhop at Joe Cotton's that would sell underage beer. Drugs were something the doctor prescribed. Teen pregnancy was a foreign affair, which means most of those torrid play-by-plays of nights at Perkerson Park were embellished. Racism was never mentioned in all-white schools or segregated neighborhoods.

Life was slow and simple. People enjoyed drive-in restaurants but knew nothing about drive-thru windows. On the telephone, fingers still did the walking and phone numbers were preceded by words like Plaza or Franklin. A Happy Meal was one young people shared just about every night with Mom and Dad — after heads were bowed and someone said the blessing.

My family must have loved Sylvan Hills because between the year I started kindergarten at Sylvan Elementary and the year I went to Georgia State University, we moved three times — and we never lost sight of Buckeye Street. We moved to 1740 Sylvan Road in 1949, when I was 5 years old. Our rambling brick home offered a basement apartment for my grandparents but they only lived downstairs a few months before moving in with another member of the family.

On my first day of school, my mother got me all dressed up and I posed for pictures with Cheryl Lyle, who lived next door. We were the same age and her mother over-dressed her, too. Snapshots preserve the image of two apprehensive, uncomfortable kids. Sylvan Elementary was two blocks away but our mothers walked us up the hill to school. It was crowded with post-war children so some kindergarten students had to go in the afternoon. Cheryl and I went in the morning and were home by lunchtime.

My family watched bulldozers clear the land that became Brewer Boulevard and the other streets that connected it with Perkerson Park. We walked them when they were paved with red clay. Our house was too large so when I was seven or eight, my Dad drew plans for a smaller place at 1778 Buckeye Street, only a short walk away. I was overjoyed when I met Don Kilpatrick and Donnie Robinson, boys that were about my age. They lived next door to each other on Melrose Drive and we became buddies. The three of us continued to be friends when my folks unexplainably built yet another house at 1784 Buckeye Street. Don, Donnie and I dodged briars in the woods, braved chiggers to pick blackberries, played in the creek and made regular trips to the drug store at Sylvan Road and Harte Drive.

There was sadness, too. My best pal was a brown-and-white cocker spaniel named Julius LaRosa — who got his name from a popular singer on Arthur Godfrey's TV show. He faithfully chased baseballs I would hit into the woods behind Mary Branan Methodist Church for as long as I would hit them.

"I never would touch one of your baseballs. They were always covered with dog slobber," Donnie Robinson told me recently, laughing at the thought of those waterlogged balls.

I remember that dog and also the night that D.L. Claborn — Gary's Dad — called and told my folks that he thought my dog had been hit by a car in front of their house. We went to the Claborn's on Sylvan Road and Gary's whole family was out in the yard. It was Julie, all right.

We hurried to a vet on Murphy Avenue. The injured dog lay at my feet on the floorboard in the backseat and when I petted him, he snarled and snapped at me. I couldn't understand why he would do that. Later, the veterinarian had to put him to sleep. I cried all the way home. Mrs. Claborn called that night to see how the dog was and how I was. That's the way people were.

Before there were shopping malls, neighborhood people dodged trolley tracks and did business on Dill Avenue.

ADVENTURE WAS FREE and imagination was a constant companion for children not yet consumed by TV. Saturdays there were bus rides to downtown for cowboy movies at the Lowe's Grand or the Paramount after a quick trip to Krystal for some of those square hamburgers. Before catching the bus home, there was time to marvel at the tricks and gadgets in a magic store across from the theaters.

Growing up in the 1950s, Herb Britt and friends created their own adventures. "Nothing was more fun than stealing a watermelon from the Farmer's Market and taking it over to Adair Park to crack it open," he confesses.

A decade later, Lee DeFore and Ronnie Dodson found other thrills. They lived in Capitol View and just about every day they passed the abandoned Sylvan Theater on Dill Avenue. Whenever they walked past, the building seemed to be inviting them inside. One day they accepted. "We crawled through an air-conditioning duct in the back of the building. When we got inside, it was dark, dusty and spooky. The seats and everything were still there," DeFore says.

To foster their daredevil reputation, DeFore and Dodson sneaked on to the perilous metal fire escape that was perched several stories up the backside of Capitol View Baptist Church. "We went inside the church and climbed out to the fire escape. We ran up and down those steps over and over," DeFore recalls.

Firefighters across the street saw what was happening and they knew how dangerous that was. The firemen put the fear of God and the law into the youngsters. "They came over and got us down and told us they were going to call the police. We were so scared that we never went on that fire escape again," DeFore laughs.

Most adventures were tamer. For Kaye and Leigh Howell, it was frequent expeditions to Perkerson Park. They lived next to the park, where Woodburne Drive butted into Fairbanks Street. Joined by friends Carol Jordan and Marilyn Martin, the Howell girls packed lunches in the baskets on the front of their bicycles and took off for the park.

When they tired of riding around the ball fields, they climbed down the steep steps to the pavilion for a picnic. Afterward, they went on jungle safaris or pretended they were cowgirls galloping up and down the hills. "I always thought I'd marry Roy Rogers," says Kaye, now Mrs. Richard Hyatt.

On days when they were not cowgirls, the girls met in the Howell's backyard and built small towns in the dirt. "That area near our garage was always dug up," Kaye says. "That was where we built our villages. We made buildings out of shoeboxes and even had little furniture inside. We stayed out there for hours. We didn't have Barney on TV, but we still had our imagination."

KIDS IN SYLVAN Hills and Capitol View shared Perkerson Park but children in a six-block neighborhood off Stewart Avenue had Adair Park all to themselves. It was their playpen, according to Pat Thomas Brannon, who loves that part of town as much as anyone.

The distinctive entranceway to Sylvan Elementary School was always a
beautiful sight.

Her father was scoutmaster so their front porch was a launching pad for neighborhood fun. Brannon's friends knew the park so well that they numbered the swings. If a friend called and said to meet them at the first swing, they knew right where to go. "We rolled out of bed, ate breakfast, then went to the park to spend the day — until Mama called from the back porch to 'come quickly' or 'right now.' You couldn't ignore the call because someone would hear her and yell that 'Your Mama is calling you'"

Adair was the school of parents as well as children. Youngsters often had the same teachers and same classrooms that their mothers and fathers had when they were kids. The school year always included colorful events such as the Halloween Carnival and the Christmas Pageant. "The pageant was complete with a recitation of the Luke Chapter 2 version of the Christmas story with references to God and Jesus and the Angel of the Lord that came upon them," Brannon recalls. "Despite those references, lightning never struck and the ACLU never darkened our doors."

The park was alive with activities, and girls were under the watchful eye of Francis Fincher. She was ahead of her time, a woman that believed little girls also deserved a chance to play. She took the girls softball team on road trips all over town. They traveled on city buses — equipment and all.

Adair kids enjoyed competing so every year they entered the Atlanta Recreation Department's kite contest and lantern parade at Piedmont Park. Brannon claims she can still put one together today if necessary. "They had to be homemade and the park furnished all the supplies. What fun it was. We'd load those beautiful lanterns on a bus and ride all the way across town. The lantern parade was at night and it was a sight to see the lanterns reflecting into the lake. The light source was a candle so a lot of lanterns ended up in that same lake after they caught fire."

A red brick building known as the Little Red House provided storage space for playground equipment and maintenance supplies. There were also restrooms for boys and girls but parents encouraged their children to stay away from them unless there was an emergency. No one mentioned a threat of sexual predators, just that the restrooms were dark and dirty.

By the mid-1950s, the recreation department added on to the Little Red House, providing space for a multi-purpose area where there was room for activities such as arts and crafts. The room was larger but it was short on charm. Brannon cherishes memories of cold, rainy afternoons she and her friends spent huddled in the original Little Red House.

"We would pile into that little storage space and sit on softball bases, jump ropes, gas cans — whatever was housed in there — and spend the afternoon reading stories or sharing what children of the day enjoyed sharing. I'm sure there was a little gas heater in there as well. Looking back, it was an accident waiting to happen. But thankfully our guardian angels prevailed," Brannon says.

SPORTS WERE ALSO important and city parks were the centerpieces. Elementary schools had Gra-Y football teams that played at Adair Park. Basketball games were held in the Girls Gym at Sylvan High. In the 1950s, boys played on city-sponsored baseball teams at Perkerson Park. It was primitive by today's Little League standards. There were no fences and no uniforms. Only a backstop made it look official.

An organized Little League program did not come to the park until the early 1960s, founded by the father of future Sylvan athletes Rick and Ray Stoeckig. The city put in dugouts and fences and Georgia Power donated lights. This program helped stock the high school with players through the 1970s.

Ronnie Dodson, a 1961 Sylvan graduate, recalls an earlier baseball team at the park. It was nothing like the well-equipped teams of today, but for Dodson it was memorable. "I must have been 10 years old. We won some kind of division and we went to a tournament in Ben Hill," he recalls. "We wore T-shirts with iron-on numbers and we rode over there in the back of a city truck. When we got there, the coach told us to wait in the truck, that he had something for us. He came back with a box of matching hats. We felt like major leaguers."

Not every memory of the park brings a smile. Larry Hampton's unforgettable day came during the summer of 1972. It started with joy and ended with unspeakable grief. Hampton was 12 years old, pitching for the Chargers after several summers on the minor league Crackers. He was on the mound at Perkerson Park as his team played for the first half championship. What a day it was for a little kid. He pitched all six innings of a 1-0 victory over the Giants. His team was the champs.

His father, Frank Hampton, sat in the stands on the first base side of home plate. It was a big day for him too. No father could be prouder than he was as he watched little Larry rack up the win.

"This is just like the World Series," he told Larry's mother.

Those were his last words.

Frank Hampton fell dead of a heart attack. The umpire tried to revive him to no avail. In an instant, the victory on the scoreboard was dwarfed by what happened near home plate. The game is forgotten but everyone remembers what happened next.

From the earliest days of the neighborhood, Perkerson Park was valued by nearby young people.

More vital than even sports were our connections to faith and religion. Traditional values were taught in just about every household. Beliefs were celebrated, not hidden under a basket. People wore their Bible Belts with pride. Churches were scattered through every neighborhood — most of them Baptist and Methodist.

As a child, I did not know a single Jewish or Catholic person. I learned firsthand of the hardships endured by a Catholic family that had a short stay on Brewer Boulevard. My father's company transferred the man of the house from Chicago. His daughter was about my age and I was supposed to make her feel at home at Sylvan High. I did not do a good job. We were called to their house one night and the girl was in tears. People at school called her names and she was crying her heart out. I was teen-aged stupid. I just sat there and listened. We were not very cosmopolitan, and though my parents tried to do what they could they did not know much more than I did about the Catholic faith. Within a few days, the girl and her mother were back in Chicago. The man followed as soon as the house sold.

So much for my diplomatic career.

THE LORD'S PRAYER was recited every morning in every homeroom at Sylvan High, followed by the pledge of allegiance to the flag of the United States of America. We closed our eyes and put our hands over our hearts. Those practices were part of our DNA. We repeated them because we believed them — and nobody threatened to take us to court.

Be glad lawyers were not around when one of my classmates conducted prayer meetings every morning in a boy's restroom on the second floor at Sylvan. John Brinsfield hoped to save the souls of wayward fellows that hung out there. Some of those guys even smoked cigarettes. Brinsfield eventually finished at Georgia Military Academy on his way to West Point. He is a U.S. Army chaplain and an instructor at Chaplain's School. The colonel's resume does not mention any other evangelistic efforts he conducted in restrooms.

Religion was part of every facet of life. We were in church with our families on Sunday mornings but on Sunday evenings we often joined friends at other churches for BTU or MYF. Whatever your affiliation, you were always welcomed.

That was the spirit in 1959 when Mary Branan Methodist Church started work on its sanctuary on Sylvan Road. For almost a decade, members worshipped in a flat-topped rock building. The Lord and the bank finally said it was time to build a church with a steeple. Kaye Howell Hyatt remembers her parents joining the work crews that helped finish the project. Children played on the church grounds while members and neighbors hammered nails and carried 2-by-4s. Her uncle, Harden Herndon, donated the bell that still hangs in the steeple.

Every Christmas, the church held a live nativity scene. For several years, Ernie and Sis Howell provided a home in their backyard on Woodburne Drive for Nelliebelle, one of the play's key cast members. Ernie was Joseph.

Sis played the role of Mary. The talented donkey usually arrived early so she could get reacquainted with her co-stars.

In the fine print of her contract, Nelliebelle was required to be a playmate for Kaye and Leigh and those girls kept her busy. While she was there, she was fed some kind of corn-based feed. It smelled so sweet and good that the Howell sisters just had to taste it for themselves. Once.

When the four-legged actor arrived in 1959, a very different Mrs. Howell greeted the animal. Like Mary, Sis was with child. That Christmas, the nativity scene had a touch of realism unlike any other when Joseph led Nelliebelle and Mary up the ramp to the roof of the original church building.

Retired Cobb County schoolteacher Harriett McDaniel Gillham also grew up at Mary Branan. In her blog, *The Other Side of the Mountain*, she describes Sundays when the Methodist served a Pot-Luck Dinner. It was held in a downstairs fellowship hall with green linoleum on the floor and Venetian blinds on the windows. She writes about her church but her descriptions apply to other nearby congregations:

> Pot-Luck! What a great name. If I was lucky, I could fill my plate over and over with the goodies brought to that hall — and I grew up in the age of the casserole. If a mother added cream of mushroom soup and sour cream to anything, it became twice as yummy! Who couldn't eat broccoli if it was covered in cheese? My own mother, a nutritionist, never served casseroles. They were of the Devil.
>
> As I think back to that hall with the long table set up on either side, covered in long white tablecloths and covered from end to end with food, it brings back nothing but good memories of watching the mothers and other ladies of the church bring bowls of salads and vegetables, plates of biscuits and corn bread, and oblong platters of fried chicken or ham covered with aluminum foil.
>
> Adhesive tape adhered to the bottom of the dishes with family last names avoided any mix up as to what plate belongs to whom. I waited patiently while the minister or a deacon drew our attention to him to bless the food.

I was always proud when my Daddy was asked to say this prayer as he had a beautiful voice, a varied vocabulary, and a way of phrasing that was a gift. I also prayed that it would be short.

I stood in line with my plate, mouth watering, the aromas of good things to come wafting in the air, and then I took my heaping plate of food to the table. If I were sitting with my friends, we saved places by placing purses or coats in chairs or turning it up to lean against the table and mark this spot as 'saved.'

Heh. Saved. Church.

Never mind.

At that table, we broke bread with our neighbors, our school friends, and our church body. We laughed, we caught up on each other's lives, and we ate large.

———

Rausey Mason was a three-year starter at Georgia Tech.

5

A Step Away from Abyss

Six or seven games into the 1964 football season, habit turned to ritual. Every week and every game the pre-game routine was the same. Beal Lazenby sat in the same seat on the team bus as he did the week before and the one next to him was reserved for Danny Eckstein. As long as the team was winning no one dared make a change.

As the team boarded the bus to the stadium, cheerleaders presented each player a stick of gum for good luck and every Friday night Lazenby stuffed his into his helmet. The Golden Bears were unbeaten, and as long as they were winning Lazenby kept stuffing his stick of gum inside his headgear.

"It was late in the year. I don't know who we were playing that night but somebody tackled Beal real hard and sticks of chewing gum flew out of his helmet. He got down on his knees and started picking up the gum off the grass. He was frantic. It was like our whole season depended on it," he remembers.

Eckstein is a professor at a medical school in the Caribbean and the author of 18 books. Decades have passed, but when he was asked about that singular season at Sylvan High funny stories were as memorable as the 10-1 campaign that team put in the record book. "As good as our record was, Ed Newby always made us feel like we were one step away from abyss," Eckstein says, remembering the approach of his head coach. "We never counted our pennies before we earned them."

At the time, that was the finest season a Sylvan High football team had ever recorded. It was the first 10 win season in school history and the first time a Bear team had played in the Milk Bowl with a city title on the line since 1953. To their chagrin, they lost to Dykes High 37-0. When the 1964 football season was history, polls ranked them the tenth best team in Georgia.

Newby, in his second season at Sylvan, was in charge of a talented group of players — with or without the sticks of gum. Joining Eckstein and Lazenby in the backfield was quarterback Donnie Hampton. Like Eckstein (Presbyterian) and Lazenby (Auburn), Hampton (Georgia) went on to play college football.

It was 12 long years before Coach Willie Hunter's 1976 Bears broke through the milestones established in 1964. His team went 11-1, was the first Sylvan squad to top statewide polls and the first to make the state playoffs. They threw a 25-0 shutout at Walter F. George in the first round but lost to Commerce 22-8 in the second round. They finished seventh in the state after spending nine weeks at No. 1.

That team was built around defensive back William Judson, running back David Allen and lineman Kenneth Collins. Each was first team All-State. Judson played at South Carolina State before a brilliant career as a cornerback with the Miami Dolphins. In seven pro seasons, he grabbed 24 interceptions and returned two for touchdowns. He is the only Sylvan product to play in the National Football League.

Hunter, later the head coach at Clark-Atlanta and Morris Brown, guided the Golden Bears to a 19-2-1 record over two seasons — the best back-to-back years in school history. Like Newby, those were Hunter's only two years at Sylvan.

The long arm of No. 59 Allen Rodgers lassoes the Benedictine ball carrier as Paul Wood rushes up to help in a 1951 game at Chaney Stadium.

WHEN THE SCHOOL opened in 1950, most people assumed the Bears would celebrate many successful seasons. Head coach Jimmy Green had been an assistant coach on Brown's state championship team so he knew how to win. His first team was beset by injuries and logistical problems but still finished a respectable 4-4-2.

The following two seasons Sylvan only won seven games though the Bears produced their first major college athlete in halfback Stan Cochran and first all-state player in tackle Rausey Mason. Both signed with Georgia Tech.

By 1953, the Bears were certified contenders. Led by fullback George Fraphart, the team finished the regular season 7-3. They earned a berth opposite Grady High in the Milk Bowl Game with a region title and city championship on the line. Erk Russell, who went on to a legendary career as an assistant coach at Georgia and head coach at Georgia Southern, was the Grady coach. The Knights topped Sylvan 21-6 with tailback Jeff Davis scoring three TDs, one on a 98-yard scamper. Grady, 11-1-1, went on to win the state Class AA title. Sylvan finished 10th in the state and was the first ranked team in school history.

Three lackluster seasons followed, but the 1957 Bears — led by co-captains Allen Johnson and Ronnie Gilstrap — finished 7-3 and tenth in the state.

The 1958 squad, paced by All-State quarterback Doug Cooper, produced the best record in school history to date, going 7-2-1. Only a crushing 18-0 loss to Northside late in the season cost the Bears another spot in the state polls.

For those of us growing up nearby, those were heady times. College football was a distant sport and pro football was only seen on TV. Fellows in the neighborhood played at Sylvan. Seeing a player in his black jacket with leather sleeves and a large gold "S" sewn on the chest was something to talk about.

Sylvan's Bobby James hugs the football on a determined run against Russell High in 1951.

My introduction to the team came through Mr. and Mrs. Glenn Hulgan, my next-door neighbors on Buckeye Street. Christine Hulgan's brother was Alvin Davis Sr. a real estate agent with Simeon L. Steed. Alvin Davis Jr. quarterbacked Sylvan teams in the mid-1950 and the Hulgans took me to see him play at Cheney Stadium.

The atmosphere was captivating. Cheerleaders danced and squealed. The band played lively music and pretty majorettes pranced down the field. I almost lost my voice screaming for Alvin Davis. The Davis boys kept Sylvan fans cheering for years. After Alvin came Richard, Don and Larry. A Davis brother was in the backfield for more than a decade.

I assumed me and my friends would some day suit up in black and gold. I had one problem: talent. I was a member of the 8th grade team in 1957 and the B-Team in the ninth and tenth grades but never got into a game. At practice one day, Coach Clem Knight called for "Oklahoma," a drill in which two linemen went nose to nose — one on defense, one on offense. The blocker was supposed to open a hole for a running back. The defensive player was supposed to tackle him.

Bodies scurried in every direction but I was too dumb to know what was happening. Guys were counting heads and pushing me up in line and I finally learned why. Across from me, larger than life, was Stewart "Moose" Davis. He was big and down in his stance he looked like a giant. On one play, he blocked and on the next play I was supposed to block Moose. We did that several times. I never blocked him and I never made a tackle. I was knocked on my rear on every play. If Coach Knight hadn't blown his whistle, I'd still be out there with Moose Davis' cleats in my face.

Then there was the Saturday morning we were playing at Murphy High. Ray Gable, one of our starting backs, had been sick and had missed school for a couple of days. He was in street clothes, watching from the sidelines as Murphy racked up a first half lead.

"Hyatt," Coach Knight yelled.

I was shocked. I didn't think he knew my name.

He did. He even called it a second time.

This was my moment, I thought. The coach is putting me in. I was already imaging how good I'd look in a lettermen's jacket — only Clem Knight was more interested in the hand-me-down uniform I was wearing.

"You're about Gable's size," the coach said. "Go over in those woods and give him your uniform."

My uniform played well in the second half. As for me, I eventually ended up sacking groceries at the Colonial Stores in Stewart-Lakewood Shopping Center. I was better at that than I was football.

Simple pieces of gold cloth generated school spirit on football Fridays.

THE 1958 SEASON was Green's final year as head football coach at Sylvan. After nine seasons and a 44-40-8 record, he became the first principal of Walter F. George High School, located adjacent to I-85 on the way to Hapeville. The hiring of his successor proved to be a full-blown controversy. Backfield coach Jack Wood and line coach Steve Vernarsky were loyal assistants under Green. Their credentials were similar, though Wood had experience as a head coach, taking Hogansville High to a 2-7-1 record in 1949.

Each applied for the Sylvan job in 1959 and citywide athletic director Sid Scarborough had a dilemma. For advice, he turned to Bill Paschal Sr., one of his greatest players at Tech High. Scarborough trusted his football knowledge and also knew that his son, Bill Paschal Jr., was a lineman at Sylvan, on his way to a fine career at Georgia Tech. For reasons now unknown, the elder Paschal recommended Wood, though Vernarsky was his son's position coach at Sylvan. Vernarsky, a fire-breather on his good days, did just what you would think he would do. He quit.

Wood's first order of business was to rebuild a coaching staff and those decisions were sound. Jack Short was hired as line coach and as backfield coach he chose Lawrence Graves. Short became head baseball coach and a year later his diamond squad came within a controversial balk call of winning the city title. Graves was head track coach and head cross country coach for many years and became one of the school's most popular teachers. Years later, after leaving Sylvan, Graves had a successful stint as head football coach at Bass High.

Wood's decisions on the field were not so sound. From 1955 to 1965, Sylvan produced some of the finest athletes in the annals of the school and some of the best in the city. That was evident by two state championships in basketball and unusual success in baseball, led by talented players such as Tommy Chapman, Beal Lazenby, Ronnie Gilstrap, Mickey Phillips, Mike Pickett, Charlie Owens and Wilson Culbreath.

In track, Brownie Thurman won the 440-yard dash in the 1956 state meet, Bill Paschal won the discus throw in 1960, Steve Copeland won the high jump in 1963 and Donald Burkett won the broad jump in 1966. Donald Hankinson won the school's only statewide tennis title in 1956 and the Rifle Team continued to bring home championship trophies. The Bears produced talent in just about every sport and the 1959 football team was no exception.

Wood inherited a core group led by All-State tackle Billy Paschal and All-City end Joe Wolfe. Each would receive football scholarships to Southeastern Conference schools — Paschal to Georgia Tech and Wolfe to Vanderbilt. At quarterback, he had Tommy Roberts and Tommy Chapman. As a tandem, they were known as "The Tommy Guns." Roberts later signed with Clemson University to play football but instead accepted a basketball scholarship to Georgia Tech. Chapman, arguably the best pitcher in school history, opted for a baseball scholarship to Clemson. He later signed with the Philadelphia Phillies and spent several years in pro baseball.

Wood had powerful runners in Alfred Spence and Charles Jordan who went to Auburn and Georgia Tech, respectively. He was likewise blessed with a group of college line prospects that included Billy Seabrook (Vanderbilt), Mack Cobb (Presbyterian) and Raymond Wilbanks and Moose Davis (UT-Chattanooga).

Despite strength upfront and a versatile offense, the team sputtered and struggled. They managed to win six of their first nine outings setting up a key game against — as you might expect — archrival Brown. With the Milk Bowl and a Region 3AAA title at stake, the Rebs won easily, 32-6. The Bears finished 6-4 — Wood's only winning season.

The 1960 team, when 17 key players were seniors, was an even more disappointing 5-5. This with a team picked to win the city title and a squad blessed with nearly 20 players that attended college on athletic scholarships. Four losses were by a total of 20 points and only a victory over Brown avoided a losing season.

Roberts remembers the unfulfilled promise.

"After our junior year we were highly-rated going into our senior year," Roberts says. "At Georgia Tech, they had a list of prospects that were invited to be on the sideline for every home game. At first, a lot of us were on that list, but there were fewer every week. We had the talent to do so much more."

In 1962, after two 4-6 seasons in a row, Wood was hanged in effigy from a goal post on the Sylvan practice field — reportedly by two of his former players. Before long, principal James C. Fain announced a change of coaches.

HIS SUCCESSOR WAS Ed Newby, an assistant football coach and successful track coach at Southwest High School. Like Wood, Newby discovered a treasure chest of talent, led by bruising fullback Lee Kidd, tackle Larry Seabrook and end Richard Munn. Kidd later started at Auburn University. Seabrook — an All-State tackle — played at Jacksonville State. Munn played at Presbyterian.

Unlike Wood, Newby knew what to do with talent. Early in the year they searched for their identity but going into the finale, the 1963 Bears had won four of five games — the only loss a one-point setback to Dykes High. They finished the season only a few yards of turf away from the Milk Bowl.

As usual, Brown was Sylvan's obstacle. The final game ended in a 6-6 tie. Using an archaic penetration rule, statisticians in the press box determined that the Rebels penetrated deeper into Sylvan territory. That meant Brown (5-4-2) went to the Milk Bowl where they lost a squeaker to North Fulton. Sylvan's season ended a deceptive 4-5-1.

Newby had to retool and rethink. Kidd, his ramrod fullback, graduated and so did Seabrook, who opened up many of the holes. But during track season, Graves told Newby about a transfer student blessed with speed a coach couldn't teach.

That would be Eckstein, who arrived from Oklahoma in the middle of his junior year. His parents were leaders in the Salvation Army, which brought his family to the headquarters on Stewart Avenue. For him, this was a chance to find a home — athletically and socially. "I hit .575 for the baseball team that spring. I didn't have a lot of power but if I hit it on the ground I could usually beat it out. I also ran track. That's where I met Coach Graves. I still remember one of his saying: 'Running track is mind over matter. I don't mind and you don't matter.' He was quite a coach," Eckstein says.

That spring he met Lazenby and Hampton. He remembers a game in which Lazenby had a no-hitter in the ninth inning only to hear the crack of the bat as an opposing hitter slammed a ball into left center field. "I ran it down, and when I caught it, Beal was halfway out there by the time I grabbed it," he recalls.

Eckstein grew up in the self-contained world of the Salvation Army and Sylvan expanded his horizons. He fit in well, and was elected president of the Senior Class in 1964. "That meant my date and I were supposed to dance the lead dance at Homecoming — and I had never danced before in my life. I found the whole milieu of high school football — the games, the pep rallies, the bonfires and the cheerleaders. I felt school spirit in a way the others didn't. My classmates and teammates had known each other since the first grade. I was the new kid."

It did not take the 8th Grade Cheerleaders long to absorb the Sylvan spirit.

Bonds created on the baseball team were important when he stepped on to the football field. His friendships with Lazenby and Hampton went deep. Down the road, he followed them and they followed him. He talks proudly of Lazenby's career as a pitcher at Auburn and how he led the Tigers with a 1.43 ERA in 1969. He talks about the quarterback controversy Hampton found himself in at Georgia and how excited he was when he heard his former teammate had officiated a Super Bowl Game. When he mentioned Hampton's death, his tone was sad. Hampton died in 1995 while on the tennis court in a double's match with his wife.

That threesome came up large in 1964. They marched through the regular season undefeated — all the way to a city championship match-up with Dykes and quarterback Billy Payne. Payne played defensive end at Georgia but made his mark as chairman of the Atlanta Olympics Games in 1996. He put together the organization that brought the Olympics to the city.

Early in the Milk Bowl showdown, Eckstein zeroed in to tackle Payne on a quarterback keeper. His shoulder was badly injured and he never made it back into the game. When it was over, Dykes had burst Sylvan' bubble with a 36-0 shellacking.

In that summer's Georgia High School All-Star Football Game, Hampton, Lazenby and Payne were teammates. Hampton threw a scoring pass to none other than Mr. Payne. For the next four years, they were teammates in Athens.

Major colleges feared Eckstein was too small but on a single afternoon, Presbyterian coach Curley Gault watched as he left a baseball game to go participate in a track meet. Gault was impressed and he invited Eckstein to play football at Presbyterian.

It was the right decision. He was named to the Little All-America football squad and as a senior returned to Atlanta to play for Penn State's Joe Paterno in the Coaches All-America Football Game. In the 1968 NFL draft, Vince Lombardi and the Green Bay Packers selected Dan Eckstein of Presbyterian College. He was the first Sylvan athlete ever drafted by the National Football League.

That summer he went to training camp with Green Bay — an experience that put him on the field with legends. "In one session, we were working in the big stadium. During a pass drill, Bart Starr laid it out there and I caught it full stride. He came down and jumped into my arms like a little kid,"

His story does not end like a fairy tale though. NFL teams were restricted to 40-man rosters and he was the 41st player. He spent a year playing in Canada and was signed by the Miami Dolphins. A hamstring injury curtailed his chances with Coach Don Shula so he entered graduate school. By the age of 26 he had his doctorate.

His brothers Dave and Doug also played at Sylvan. Dave Eckstein was a running back. Following his older brother to Presbyterian, he blossomed and became the school's first 1,000-yard rusher. Doug Eckstein was a tight end in 1971 and later played on Carson-Newman's national championship team. At Sylvan, Eckstein's brothers celebrated few victories. After that 10-1 record in 1964, the Bears suffered losing records nine out of the next 10 seasons.

THEN CAME WILLIE Hunter and Sylvan's finest moments, though some of his players remember more than victories. Hunter wanted his players to be in shape so every day they ran five or 10 laps around the practice field. Two of his players, Roger Noble and David Paul, figured out a way to escape that running.

"We would wait until the coaches weren't looking and we run over the hill and go to Parramore's. They had the best Cherry Cokes," Noble recalls. "We were so thirsty that to this day I believe those were the best drinks I have ever had. After the Cherry Cokes, we would sneak back up and wait for a chance to rejoin the team as they were running laps."

Despite their escapades, Hunter's 1975 team was 8-1-1 and embarked on a 15-game winning streak that extended into the 1976 campaign. The Bears were eighth in the state but Hunter was not through. His 11-1 Bears advanced to the second round of the 1976 playoffs before losing to Commerce High 22-8 in an upset at Lakewood Stadium. His record as a high school coach at Sylvan and Fulton was 94-31-2. He later coached at Clark-Atlanta but his record there was not so outstanding. He was fired in 1997 after a 30-40-1 record over eight seasons.

Hunter's teams were the last ones that made Sylvan cheer. By 1978, the Bears were 0-10 — the only winless season in school history. Football historians cannot identify the name of the head coach that season and neither does the 1978 *Golden Memories*. There were momentary successes in the coming years but the school had greater concerns than football.

Neighborhoods around the school were aging without grace and enrollment was declining. New high schools were being built around Atlanta and old ones were being discarded. Sylvan High closed after the 1986-1987 school year and reopened as a middle school. More than three decades of football came to a quiet conclusion. A program that began with promise and potential was shut down without achieving the elusive championship it wanted so badly so long.

Thirty-six years of football produced 171 victories, 187 losses and 15 ties. Despite the individual talent that it put on the field, only one Sylvan team won a region title. Exciting moments were celebrated, but negatives always blocked the paths to glory. So did Northside, Murphy and North Fulton. Sylvan's all-time records against those schools was 2-17, 3-15-1 and 4-12, respectively. Many of those setbacks occurred at crucial points of the season, too.

It came down to one season and one game.

Ronald Brown had been Sylvan's football coach since 1979. In his first seven years, he managed just two winning seasons. His eighth year in charge would be his third. The Bears finished 6-4, and, appropriately, their goodbye game was at rickety old Chaney Stadium on November 21, 1986.

When the lights at the stadium were turned off after that final outing, a Sylvan High team of another generation, composed of players whose skin was a different color, hung up their black and gold jerseys for the last time. Years before, Stan Cochran scored the school's first TD and that night, in the third period, Corey Watson ran into the end zone for Sylvan's final six points. That group of Golden Bears finished what the 1950 squad started. They defeated East Atlanta 6-0.

———

Freddy Recher's enduring love of Sylvan sports was contagious

6

What a Wonderful School to Me

F reddy Recher no longer waddled on to the football field with water spilling out of his bucket and school spirit pouring down his face. He was living in an assisted living facility when some old friends from high school came to visit. His mind no longer focused and his body was shutting down, but they talked about the old days and they talked about Sylvan High.

Around the school and around sporting events, Freddy was a fixture. Students graduated and teachers retired, but he was always there, doing what had to be done. For decades, he prowled the sidelines at Sylvan High football games and when it was time for basketball he was always courtside. No one loved that school more than he did.

Photographs that captured the celebration that followed a state championship include Freddy, running on to the court. A few minutes after tournament officials presented the trophy to Coach Ozzie Wadewitz, pictures were taken. In one of them, *Atlanta Constitution* sports editor Jesse Outlar symbolically handed the oversized award to the Sylvan coach. Ozzie then asked the cameraman to take a second photo with Freddy holding the coveted award.

No one could have been more proud.

Generations of Sylvan people remembered Freddy Recher and the 1973 edition of *Golden Memories* presented this well-deserved salute: "He is a symbol of dedication for our team. He devotes himself to any task, even if it is just giving water to the players during a break. It is this spirit and devotion that makes us proud to know Freddy Recher, and to show him our gratitude for a job well done."

His devotion to the school began long ago. That's why Herb Britt and players from some of Sylvan's earliest football teams went to see him a few years before his death. His health was in decline. His face had no emotions and he said very little until someone suggested they all sing the Sylvan Fight Song. Freddy's face brightened, and in a strong, clear voice he sang every word of a song he loved.

Oh! Here's to Sylvan High.
Oh! What a wonderful school to me.
Sylvan High, your name will live in history.
We will fight for your honor, and sing for your fame;
Carry the glory of Sylvan High's name.
Oh! Here's to Sylvan High.
The team will break right through the line
To win the game each time.
So take your hats off to the fighting black and gold team
And stand and cheer for Sylvan High.

THAT IS NOT A song you hear very often anymore. Bootleg CDs of old Sylvan band concerts are sometimes passed around and at class reunions — after celebrating the social hour — nostalgic graduates stumble through the words and offer off-key renditions of a song that will always top the Sylvan High Hit Parade

Robert Jenkins, the school's first band director, adapted the melody from a classical piece. His wife added original lyrics. The Sylvan band introduced it in 1958 and the rousing song became an overnight tradition. From then on, it was the most requested song at pep rallies, bon fires and football games. When Sylvan people heard the opening notes no one had to ask them to stand and cheer.

Dianne Ferguson Crawford caught the spirit at her first pep rally and for five years she was a Sylvan cheerleader. She was a member of the 1961 varsity squad that included Edna Johnson, Sandra Link, Mary Sweatman, Linda Lockbaum, Crawford, Diane Paschal, Pat Kerlin, Patty Lotz and Mary Jane Casey.

Jenkins and his wife also collaborated on a more somber song — the Sylvan Alma Mater. He had arrived as part of the original faculty and served as the school's band director until 1961. Jenkins' student musicians provided background music for the early years of the school and helped foster a spirit that old grads still talk about.

THAT SPIRIT HELPED Dianne Ferguson Crawford survive her first day as an eighth grader. She was 12 years old and she was scared. "They announced we would be having a pep meeting that afternoon and I did not want to go sit in an any old meeting. I tried to get out of it by staying in English class but they said everyone had to go. Well, when I walked into the gym to the band playing *Rock Around the Clock*, I was bitten by the Golden Bear spirit," says Crawford, a member of the Class of 1961.

Fred Piper rocked around the clock at home. His older sister Janice was a Twirlette at Sylvan and as a child he remembers Eleanor Woodall, Emily Warner and his sister practicing that routine in his family's front yard for hours. "I never understood why until I saw them in action. Those girls could rock!" he recalls. "I watched them go up and down the field at football games and it didn't matter if the Golden Bears won or not. You hoped it would be as you remembered it when you got to those great big doors to the entrance of the gym your first day of eighth grade."

Sometimes being in the band was a problem. Doug Newman was in Jack Elder's class in the ninth grade and when he kept beating on his desk, the Social Studies teacher made him pick up his desk and take it into the hall. After a while, Elder came out there and suggested the young man take up a band instrument.

"I'm already in the band," Newman said.

"What do you play?" the teacher asked.

"The drums."

The only thing the longtime teacher could do was roll his eyes. Mr. Elder had just thrown Brer Rabbit into the briar patch.

Like so many others, Newman's memories of Sylvan revolve around teachers, not the schoolhouse. Years later, the building is a symbol of the classmates and teachers that roamed the halls when old grads were young and foolish. As students they were stuck in puberty and teachers forgave them their trespasses and ignored their weaknesses.

D.W. Heidecker could not have known it then, but teachers in that first group he hired were building blocks. The nucleus of that that first faculty and staff welcomed other teachers into the fold along the way and until the end Sylvan was blessed with educators that understood the original mission.

Through the years, it was an interesting group.

- Miss Ruth Rogers must have been born with white hair tied up in a bun on the back of her head. After retiring she earned a doctor of divinity degree from Emory University and was a fulltime Methodist minister. If someone talked out of turn in her class, she said, "Anyone with permission to talk, stand on your head."
- James Wash parked his dilapidated old car in the back of the school for many years. It was filled with stale cigarette smoke and personal eccentricities. Not even his smartest student could figure out a way to remove the nicotine stains from the science teacher's fingers.
- The Wadewitz family made themselves at home. Ozzie was there for the first day of school and in 1952 his brother Richard joined him on

the coaching staff. He stayed four years. Ozzie's wife Rosemary was the first school secretary.

- Mrs. Virginia McCord taught English when she was not counting — and counting — and counting — the books she obsessively arranged on her desk. She was the brunt of mischief for many years. On one occasion, students threw her reference books out the window of her second floor classroom. Rufus Burger, whose class was below her, watched them float by his window and returned the books to her desk.

- Miss Norma Fields was her name when she arrived in 1954 but most students remember her as Mrs. Norma McLendon. She taught there for 25 years, was the longtime advisor of *The Bear Facts* and struck fear in the hearts of senior English students. Several of her students found careers in journalism.

- Mrs. Frankie Jackson, who always seemed to wear an ensemble that included a string of white pearls and a pair of white gloves, looked like she was going to a Sunday School social instead of math class.

- Rufus Burger was an Army interpreter in World War II and he kept trying to bring a dead language to life.

- Anne Garrard managed the main office for several principals and Jane Savage was the school nurse for 19 years. When she died in 1981, the yearbook said Savage "listened with ears that heard more than words."

- Norman Silver guided the soccer team to the state playoffs in 1973 and also made history. Student Pam Walker was the first female in the country to join an all-male soccer team.

- Charles Adair helped students in his special electronics classes build 5-tube radios and also trained them to work on the school's phone system.

- She joined the faculty as Ellen Roberts but retired as Ellen Cormeier. She taught science, and many of her students actually learned the subject. When she got upset, her favorite comment was "shoot a monkey."

- Karl Kimbrough taught students the "reverse lever," a personal theory that helped them subtract negative numbers. If they wanted to learn, he encouraged them to spend half an hour a day reviewing what they did in class. (One of his students, Mark Argo, repeats those same things to his own math students today.)

- Jeff Clements, in his monotonous voice, taught Georgia history until the school closed its doors and his loyalty to the school was history making in itself. Behind his back, students called him Fred Flinstone.
- Lawrence Graves is remembered fondly as a teacher and a coach. People that no longer remember the combination to their locker or where their homeroom was still recite his homilies. He was also an outstanding track coach, mentoring teams that won more than 87 percent of their meets in a 30-year career at Sylvan, Bass and Southside. In 2004, Graves was inducted into the Georgia Athletic Coaches Association Hall of Fame.

His 1969 cross-country team was undefeated in dual meets on its way to a city and a state title. That state championship was the only one earned by a Sylvan team other than the two state basketball titles. That team, mostly juniors, was composed of Randy Owen, Ronny Johnson, Paul Foster, Eddie Allen and Mike Ferguson. They finished second in the state in 1970, coming up five points shy.

Like other coaches and teachers, Graves endured some unusual events, such as the day Johnny Copeland tried to eat his way to a medal. Copeland threw the shot put, discus and javelin and during a break in action of the state meet at Grady Stadium a family friend took him to lunch at a nearby Krystal. Asking Copeland if he was hungry was like asking a frog if it was green. He started with 10 Krystal hamburgers and a big Coke — and was far from through. Before it was over, he consumed 35 Krystals and two more large drinks.

Poor Johnny. He didn't feel well, and there were more events to go. But 35 Krystals or not, he returned to the meet and finished third in all three afternoon events — though when Graves found out about his menu, he was not happy. "Coach Graves was an awesome coach and he was always there when someone needed him — or when I needed him for support. He inspired me so much," Copeland says.

Margaret Callaway Mahan, one of the school's most beloved educators, was inducted into the Georgia Teacher Hall of Fame in 1973. In 1957, she was sponsor of the sub-freshman class. Her civics class conducted a political experiment that resulted in the election of Robert Whitmore as treasurer of the eighth grade class. There was one minor problem. He did not exist.

Robert Jenkins' student ensembles always made beautiful music and
the orchestra in 1958 was no exception. Members of that group were
James Altwies, Becky Bragg, Buddy Cochran, Jo Daniel, Roy Huff, Bobby Keith,
Margie Kitchens, Bill Legg, Ann Lee, Pat McKay, George Propes, Phillip Snell,
Walter Swearinger, Daniel Swearinger, Eddie Trainer, Jim Williams, James Winslett,
Anita Black, Elaine Buice, Marie Dorsey, Bobby Gallagher, Marguerite Laughlin,
Elaine Hagan, Muriel Laughlin and Judy Roberts.

Elections were early in the school year so incoming students did not know
one another. But soon the halls were soon filled with Whitmore's campaign
posters and classmates wore colorful buttons with his name on them. On the
day candidates delivered campaign speeches, a "friend" explained that Robert
was sick. He told voters that the candidate promised to have a pool party at
his parents' house if he was elected.

It was a landslide.

Robert Whitmore was elected.

I finished fourth.

And we never had that pool party.

TEACHERS LIKE MRS. Mahan are part of Sylvan's memory bank. They educated
their students but they taught them much more than how to diagram a sentence
or how to solve a algebra formula. They brought stability to young lives at a
time stability was desperately needed.

Stability began in the principal's office. The private room where the principal worked was by invitation only and it did not require an RSVP. Students

dispatched there did not relish that opportunity — especially if their parents were included. But the stability and continuity of the leadership provided by the administrators was important.

Heidecker set the bar high. He was promoted to Area Superintendent in 1956 and was replaced by veteran educator James C. Fain. A native of Fort Gaines, Ga., Fain joined the Atlanta school system in 1937. Prior to Sylvan, he was principal at Clark Howell and I.N. Ragsdale elementary schools.

The 1957 yearbook staff said Fain fostered the spirit of Sylvan: "With sympathetic understanding, intense interest, and personal concern for the students and faculty, he has promoted the feeling of friendship and accomplishment among all of us."

James C. Fain was the second principal of Sylvan High.

Fain was promoted to Director of Curriculum Development for the school system and Gerald Culberson, a member of the school's original faculty, replaced him in 1964. His successor was B.F. Johnston, a former football coach at Fulton High.

But whoever the chief administrator was, students relied on the teachers. "The warmth you felt from the teachers and the sense of community they had for one another was evident. It made you want to go to school every day," Pat Brannon describes.

Memories of teachers never go away. Former students complain about how hard geometry under Floyd Hendrix was and they laugh about Coach Lawrence Graves saying they were so slow they couldn't catch a Bear in a phone booth. They whine about school lunches and remember field trips to the Nabisco plant where they gave away free cookies. They remember English teacher Lita Wimpey responding to students who said, *"you know"* with a sarcastic *"We don't know. Explain."*

Wanda Jacob Rogers remembers the horrible yellow outfits girls had to wear for physical education classes. She's not alone. Other female graduates share her disdain for unfashionable garb that Rogers calls hideous.

"I weighed about 85 pounds and the teacher gave me one that was big enough to put four of me in. I refused to dress out and I got In School Suspension. Mama wouldn't listen to me and she tore my tail up. I still wouldn't wear it and I finally took the outfit home so she could see it. She had a fit. She said we could all fit in that thing. She went to the school and had it out with everybody. I finally got one to fit. I still detest that outfit," she says.

My memories are of gratitude.

It starts with Virginia Slate. She was a French teacher by trade. Why she was teaching English I don't know — but I'm thankful she was. From the beginning, she told us we would do a lot of writing that year and one day, without warning, she told us to get out pen and paper and write an essay on our favorite character in *Silas Marner.*

Ooooops! I knew I should have been reading that book. She assigned nightly readings but every night I had better things to do. Instead of embarrassed I felt smug. With a smirk, I wrote about Will Shakespeare, a fictional neighbor of Mr. Marner.

I handed in the essay and didn't think about it again until our next class. Mrs. Slate had graded our papers but before returning them she was going to read a couple of them. When I recognized my words, I slid down in my desk and prepared myself to be ridiculed. When people laughed, I assumed they were laughing at me and not my words and I was flabbergasted when Mrs. Slate told the class this was the first theme she had ever given an A-plus.

"But don't ever do this again," she whispered as she dropped my paper in front of me.

My life was upside down at that time. My troubles went beyond her class. I didn't know where I was going and really didn't care. But for just a moment someone reached me. I wanted to do well for Mrs. Slate, even if I didn't care about me. Because she cared, she discovered a talent in me that no one else had recognized.

The next school year, Norma McLendon unexpectedly invited me to write for *The Bear Facts*. I began to think about my life and what I was going to do with it. Maybe they were right, I could write.

When yearbooks came out I went to Virginia Slate's room. What she wrote in my *Golden Memories* became an unanswered challenge. She scribbled that when I wrote my first book, she wanted me to sign it for her.

When my first book was published in 1977, I did.

THOSE EXAMPLES OF school spirit were not experienced in pep rallies but they are a side of school that encourages former students every day of our lives, even if we don't realize it.

But feelings conjured up by that old fight song are also important. Around the time it was first played, the Golden Bear came to life in the person of Len Miller. No one is sure whether it was the brainchild of Miller or band director Robert Jenkins but the mother of Sylvan basketball star Jimmy Woodall, a classmate of Miller, made the costume.

"The suit might have been Len's idea because he had more spirit than anybody else," says Pat Thomas Brannon. Years later, after hanging up his bear suit, Len "Snuffy" Miller became a record producer in Nashville and the drummer for country singer Bill Anderson's Po' Boy Band.

Ray Abernathy's view of that furry golden bear is more twisted than Brannon's. A 1959 Sylvan graduate, he is a public relations consultant and speechwriter in Washington, D.C., and the author of two books. His 2007 novel, *Dirty Billy*, offers a tilted version of growing up in Sylvan Hills in the 1950s.

The scenes Abernathy sets are real. He mentions familiar streets and landmarks and recreates his old high school. Names of people are altered, to protect the innocent and the guilty. The school principal is not Mr. Heidecker. It is Mr. Heideckle. The head coach is Jimmy Brown, not

Jimmy Green. The line coach is not Steve Vernarsky. It is Coach Burski, a woodworking teacher.

At Abernathy's fictional school, Billy Wilson is determined to be Sylvan's first male cheerleader. He was a hit at tryouts and the moment arrives when the cheerleading squad is announced. Once names are posted, Mr. Heideckle calls Billy into his office. Here is Billy's account of what the principal said and did:

> I fashioned a compromise, which I caution you to accept with enthusiasm. I've been thinking for some time that we need an official mascot, not like the dumpy Winston Churchill dog they use at the university, and certainly not like the hopped-up rattletrap car they drive around at the Tech games, but an animal, not a real animal, but a furry Golden Bear who dances and prances and helps bring the team on the field and puts some puff in our stuff, some teeth in our tongues, some rowl in our growl.
>
> By this time, Mr. Adrian Heideckle was standing behind his desk and demonstrating how a Golden Bear should move and pose and dance. Then he broke into a fractured rendition of our fight song:
>
> *Glory, glory to old Sylvan*
> *Glory, glory to old Sylvan*
> *Glory, glory to old Sylvan*
> *and to hell with Joe Brown High.*
>
> Well, we can't exactly say the hell part, but you get the idea. Mr. St. Clair (the band director) will be your consultant and work with you on routines. I've made arrangements with Melissa Quinn, Mary Ann's mother, to design a costume, and you are to report to her house over on Brandywine Street this afternoon I want you ready to perform by our first home game three weeks from today when meet Grady ...
>
> The role I have created for you is far bigger than that of an ordinary cheerleader. There are twelve of them. There will

be one of you. You will be the first Golden Bear and fame will follow you."

To show younger graduates how the world has changed, Brannon recalls a Friday afternoon in 1957 when Sylvan cheerleaders cavorted into the school gym for a pep rally in short skirts for the first time. Until then, their skirts were modestly long. Cheerleaders had traditionally worn their uniforms to classes on the day of a pep meeting, but on that particular day the dignified principal asked them not to dress out unti later.

"We had gone to Mr. Fain and asked him about the idea of short skirts that summer," she recalls. "It was probably because the Northside cheerleaders were wearing them. They were trendsetters. We were followers. Mr. Fain finally said yes, but he warned us that if the public didn't take to them, we'd have to go back to our old skirts."

And one more thing, girls ...

"You can't put your names on your tights."

No one complained about the length of the skirts and a few years later, the Class of 1966 had a dose of that same school spirit. The class presented the school a five-foot bear created by Atlanta sculptor Julian Harris. It was made of a material similar to Styrofoam and six coats of epoxy were applied before it was sprayed with bronze paint. It had a place of honor in the lobby outside the principal's office for many years.

BUT THE SPIRIT of love and affection for the school was never more evident than in the two years that Sylvan earned trips to the state AAA basketball championships. Post-game parties became an instant tradition during the school's second run to the tournament.

Sandy Thames Kicklighter, a 1963 graduate, remembers passing the hat during games to pay for that night's gathering. Her parents even agreed to host one of the shindigs. "Mother, being the mother that she was, had a huge sheet cake made in the shape of a basketball court with little players in black and gold uniforms," Kicklighter says.

Dianne Ferguson Crawford was a varsity cheerleader during those magical seasons and her parents were the gracious hosts of the year's most ambitious post-game celebration. In 1961, Sylvan played two high-voltage teams from Kentucky. After the game with the Ashland Tom Cats, the Blue Grass visitors were invited to join Sylvan players at a party at the Ferguson's. It was a night where the concept of school spirit was stretched to the limit.

"Our neighbors didn't know what to think when a Greyhound bus pulled up in front of our house that night and two basketball teams started pouring out of it. My parents were pretty good sports to serve more than 200 folks. There were so many people in our little house that folks were sitting on the side of the bathtub."

———

On the bench, Ozzie Wadewitz seldom lost his cool. He was into the game and so was Charles Robinson (left) and Ronnie Dodson.

7

The Butcher's Boys

L ike most small towns in the state of Wisconsin, the Village of Slinger relied on a diet of beer, brats and basketball. Its given name was Schleisingerville and at one time this little town settled by German immigrants had as many breweries as it did banks. A stein of beer demanded a bratwurst and at Otto Wadewitz's Meat Market on Franklin Street sausages were always freshly made.

Wadewitz opened his original meat market around 1900 and his sons, Oswin and Alfred, operated it after their father retired in 1930. Oswin, a veteran of World War I, worked behind the meat counter and his family lived upstairs over the shop.

Oswin and Elda Wadewitz had three children — Oswin Jr., Richard and Bessie. Their neighborhood was zoned for working and living. Near the meat market were St. John's Evangelical Church, Wild's Furniture Company, Slinger Hardware and the Slinger Cash Food Market.

Among the people of this town, 32 miles from Milwaukee, Oswin Wadewitz was known for baseball and basketball as well as bratwurst. He played on town teams that represented Slinger in hardscrabble leagues that offered momentary escape from a Depression that hit Main Street as hard as Wall Street.

Oswin wanted his sons to know more than the family recipe for Bavarian sausage. He coached them in basketball and baseball and provided them a place to play. Back of the market a multi-purpose building served as a garage and a place to slaughter pigs. But there was more to it than that.

Nailed to the side of the building was a basketball hoop where the boys played when the weather allowed it. On the top floor was a primitive indoor basketball court. Without realizing it, their father was preparing Ozzie and Richard for what became the family profession. That profession brought Ozzie Wadewitz to Sylvan High in 1950 and two years later coaching brought his brother to town. Sylvan did not have its own gym but playing under poor conditions was nothing new to the Wadewitz boys.

UNLIKE THE SOUTH, where football borders on a religion, basketball dominated life in Wisconsin. At Sylvan, football came first. Falls were pleasant and winters mild so there was time to practice and play. Besides, boys with a Southern accent dreamed of strapping on a chinstrap by the time they were weaned.

Back in Slinger, there was no organized football. Severe winters made that decision easy and so did the cost of fielding a football team. Boys played basketball, and in the 1930s many of them came to Franklin Street to play on that makeshift court behind the butcher shop.

"We had to warm our hands over the coffee pot before we played," Dick Wadewitz says. "It wasn't modern, but it was a chance to play."

And the Wadewitz boys never stopped playing. They played in high school. They played in college, and Ozzie even played a season of semi-pro ball. They coached championship teams in high school and Dick, the younger of the two, also enjoyed a career as a college head coach. But none of their stops brought more pure joy than the days they spent playing a simple game under simple circumstances.

"It wasn't organized. There weren't any grownups out there telling us what to do. It was just a game. I was the younger brother, but Ozzie let me tag along when he played. He was always a much better player than me."

When they were young, the high school principal in Slinger recognized how important basketball was to his students so he bent the rules. If one of the boys came to his house, he gave them a key to the gym. Sometimes Dick, the youngest of the group, was given that assignment. "The principal didn't worry about restrictions," he says. "You could do those things in a small town.

Sometimes, the school janitor would see the lights on in the gym. He'd come over and run us out. We didn't care, as long as we got to play."

Sheboygan is hardly a Mecca of basketball today but in the 1930s that Wisconsin city was a breeding ground for pro basketball. The Red Skins — named for a popular sausage — played teams from industrial centers in the Midwest and eventually joined a pro league that would one day be part of the original National Basketball Association. Strange as it may seem, in the embryonic years of the NBA, Sheboygan was one of the dominant franchises.

Oswin and his two sons traveled to games in Sheboygan as often as they could. For the boys it was a chance to see professionals play the game. It also was a chance to steal ideas they would file away for later use. "That's where Ozzie got that two-handed set shot of his. He copied it from a guy that played for Fort Wayne. He learned a left-handed hook shot from another player we watched. We even saw John Wooden play one time," Dick recalls.

After high school, Ozzie went to what is now the University of Wisconsin-Milwaukee. He lettered in basketball in 1943. Then, like so many others his age, he enlisted in the U.S. Navy. He was accepted into an officer-training program and commissioned an ensign. During World War II, he served on a Landing Ship Infantry (LCI) in the Pacific, delivering foot soldiers directly to the beach while dodging enemy fire. He also played on some big-time Naval basketball teams.

After the war, he enrolled at Wheaton College, a Protestant institution in Illinois whose most renowned graduate is the Rev. Billy Graham. Wadewitz also restarted his college basketball career and was joined by little brother Richard.

Around this time, post-war America was jumpstarting what is known as Baseball's Golden Age. During the war, major league rosters had been filled with players past their prime and others that would not have been in the big leagues if the stars had not gone to war. Name players reclaimed their jobs in 1946 and clubs began restocking their far-reaching farm systems.

Ozzie Wadewitz, recognizing the eternal market for left-handed pitchers, dreamed of a baseball career. So when he heard the New York Yankees were having an all-day tryout camp near Wheaton, he and his brother went. Ozzie signed a contract with baseball's most prestigious organization and was assigned to Grand Forks in the Class C Northern League.

The 1947 Yankees were building a dynasty but none of that talent found its way to South Dakota. The Chiefs limped to a 28-92 record and are called the all-time worst team in the 38-year history of the league. Ozzie was 3-7 with an ERA of 4.62. The following season he was back in Class C and once again had problems with his control. He split time between Grand Forks and Duluth with an inauspicious record of 5-6. He lost a pitching duel with Don Larsen — known for the perfect game he pitched for the Yankees in the 1956 World Series.

Wadewitz had a 9-12 mark in 1949 — his final year in baseball. He was 2-7 with a sparkling 1.88 ERA in Class D Carrollton, Ga., and 7-5 with the Class C team in Greenville, Ms. His three-year record was 17-25.

But a victory in Mississippi did not show up in the box score. "As a pitcher, I was always around .500," Wadewitz once told an Atlanta reporter. "But my biggest victory was getting Rosemary Foresman, a young lady from Greenville, to say 'yes.' Met her while I was pitching in the Cotton States League."

They met at the ballpark. Rosemary's father and mother were baseball fans and they frequently went to games in Greenville. Her folks began inviting the quiet young man over for home-cooked meals and Ozzie and Rosemary have been together more than 60 years.

AFTER THE 1949 season, newlyweds Ozzie and Rosemary moved to Slinger. They lived with his parents and he commuted to Wheaton College to finish his degree in physical education and to complete his teaching credentials. He also played semi-pro basketball with the Milwaukee Bright Spots.

As he shopped for a job, he was offered a spot at a high school in Colorado. The salary was not impressive and Rosemary openly supported a move to the South. Someone at Wheaton referred him to a graduate of the college that was personnel director for the Atlanta school system who described an opening at the city's new high school.

What happened before the start of school is lost in time. But Wadewitz was not the first head basketball coach assigned to Sylvan. That spring, citywide Athletic Director Sid Scarborough announced the hiring of Paul Hoffman, a former All-Big 10 player at Purdue University and a six-year veteran of the NBA.

That Scarborough tabbed a basketball man is impressive. In a football-dominated city, basketball jobs often went to assistant football coaches. They did not always understand the nuances of basketball but this was a way for the school system to boost their pay. With Hoffman and Wadewitz, that was not the case.

Hoffman, a native of Jasper, Ind., played for the Baltimore Bullets, New York Knickerbockers and Philadelphia Warriors. In 1948, he sparked the Bullets to an NBA title and the year before the opening at Sylvan, he averaged 14.4 points a game for Baltimore.

After accepting the Sylvan job, he changed his mind and returned to pro basketball. When he did retire, he was general manager of the Bullets for two seasons. He later went back to Purdue as assistant basketball coach and head baseball coach. Hoffman's younger brother John did come to Atlanta a little later. He was a teammate of All-American Roger Kaiser at Georgia Tech in 1960.

Ozzie and Rosemary arrived for the first day of school at Sylvan in 1950. He taught PE and she was the school secretary. He was head basketball coach but there was one problem: There was no place to play. When it was time for tryouts, he had to shop around for a gym to use at the same time other coaches were conducting tryouts of their own.

Bobby Ward remembers that week. "When I tried out for that first Sylvan team, I had to catch a trolley and ride to the old Fulton High School near Pryor Street. It was a long ride. But I didn't have to worry about it very long. Ozzie cut me."

Wadewitz and his first band of Bears played no home games and practices had to be held at night at Fulton, Russell or Brown. There would not be a gymnasium at Sylvan until 1954.

Earl Shell has not forgotten those days without a gym. At 5-foot-6, 125 pounds, he was a boy playing with the big guys when he started practicing with the varsity as a freshman. Practices were at Fulton High on Fulton Street on property where Atlanta Stadium was built a decade later. Younger players had to catch a ride with a senior or anybody that had a car.

"It was a rough place to play. The baskets were hung from metal supports attached to a brick wall. When you drove to the basket you had to be careful or you'd end up crashing into that wall," Shell says.

Practices were well planned but Shell remembers there was time for he and the head coach to work their way around the key shooting set-shots — a game Wadewitz usually won.

"He had these special eye-glasses that were made so you couldn't look down at the floor when you were dribbling. We put them on when we worked on ball handling," says Shell, retired CEO of an Atlanta construction company.

Every game was a road game. The opening of the gym in May 1954 was welcomed. There was a proper ribbon cutting, the kind of ceremony politicians love. But it was two years before there was a celebration Wadewitz could appreciate.

Shell was a senior in 1956, Sylvan had a gym of its own by that time and the Bears enjoyed a promising season. The lineup included Shell, Gerald Hawkins, Carl Duvall, team captain Sammy Chester and either Posey Davis or Clifford Cleveland. The highlight was a weekend trip to Savannah early in the season with teams from Brown and North Fulton. "We won both of our games in Savannah," Shell says. "Looking back, we may have peaked too early. We lost in the city tournament, and we shouldn't have."

With Shell and Duvall leading the way, Sylvan defeated Roosevelt 44-37 to take the City South title for the first time in school history. A 44-43 loss to Brown in the finals of the city tournament kept the Golden Bears out of the state tournament.

Wadewitz's style of coaching fit his German heritage. Practice was organized. There was time to work and time to play but no time to waste. His sidelines were orderly and so was he. Many coaches stayed on their feet and waved their arms. Wadewitz sat calmly. He stood up if a time out was warranted. His rules were stern but few, mainly reminding players to be selfless and not selfish.

His final Sylvan team did not hear him curse until the state tournament of their senior year. When Tommy Roberts zipped a behind-the-back pass into the bleachers, Wadewitz uttered, "Dammit, Tommy." In the huddle, a shocked group of ball players looked at each other and started to laugh.

Ozzie laughed too.

His teams mirrored their coach. Guards were taught the two-handed set shot. Big guys worked on a hook shot. Players were exposed to the archaic art of shooting free throws underhanded. Early in his career, he insisted every player use that style. In his latter years, he relaxed that rule.

He could also teach his players to shoot a jump-shot, as Frank Applegate recalls. "We went out on that court in back of the school and he taught me the jump-shot when only a few people had one," says Applegate, an early Sylvan star that now lives in Arvada, Colorado. But like so many others, Applegate remembers more than basketball. "He was such a great Christian coach. He actually influenced me to teach and coach. Ozzie was the best I ever played for."

Once Alexander Memorial Coliseum opened in 1956, Georgia Tech frequently sent Wadewitz blocks of tickets for home games. "To decide who would get those tickets, we shot free throws," Steve Copeland says. "If Ozzie wanted to go a particular game, he would get in line and shoot himself. And he always won."

Sometimes the coach was challenged to get out there with the guys. Like a day at practice when Terry Stephens was so full of himself that he told the coach if he could do things better, then come on. "He was a little man like me coming up so he knew all the moves. If I fell back, he hit that set-shot of his. If I moved in on him, he used that herky-jerky stuff to get to the basket. He left me dragging," Stephens admits.

As much as anyone, Stephens studied his coach's textbook of basketball. But there was always time to compete. "I tried to beat him in a game of H-O-R-S-E for five years and it took me until my senior year to beat him," he says.

Ozzie got a free ride after winning the state title in 1960.

BUT SOMETHING FAR more important than basketball was going on in the personal lives of Ozzie and Rosemary Wadewitz. In 1951, they welcomed daughter Karen into their lives. She brought joy, followed by tragedy. Oxygen deprivation left Karen severely handicapped with no hope of recovery. This was an era when mental health professionals felt helpless treating mentally challenged children. Doctors advised them to institutionalize her, telling them Karen would never be able to function.

Ozzie and Rosemary did not listen to the medical community. Karen was their daughter. They loved her. They believed she deserved more than a dreary existence in a sterile hospital. They wanted her at home — and home is where Karen stayed.

"We couldn't hide her," Ozzie once said. "She is who she is."

Ozzie and Rosemary believed in her and they never gave up. When one could not care for her the other one did. Sylvan was her second home. Karen came to basketball practice. She attended games. Basketball players over the years were her extended family, her big brothers.

Ozzie and Rosemary became consistent voices for young people that could not speak. They became strong advocates for special education and for the rights of the mentally challenged.

Karen Melinda Wadewitz died in 2001. She was 51 years old. A monument bench in her honor was added to a garden at Peachtree Road United Methodist Church, put there by two parents that never stopped believing.

Years after he left Sylvan, Ozzie and Rosemary were blessed with a second daughter. Angela Katherine was born in 1965. Growing up, Angie Chesin became a gym rat in other gyms, primarily at Atlanta's Northside High School, where her father coached until his retirement.

"I grew up in a gym. I learned to run the clock and I can keep score. I can do it all," Angie says. Today, Clay, her 12-year-old son, is a gifted baseball player just like his grandfather was.

"He comes by that naturally," she says.

Others know Ozzie Wadewitz as a coach but not Angie. "He was just my Dad, doing what he could do to raise my sister and me."

She is proud of her parents' love for her sister and the love they have given her. She is also proud of what they have accomplished. Rosemary retired as a secretary to the top brass at Delta Airlines. She was known as a person that got things done.

Angie is proud of her father's career at Sylvan and Northside, though what she knows about his early years comes through stories others have told her. Her father is a reader, not a talker, so at home his past success was never glorified.

HIS PINNACLE AS a basketball coach was not reached without planning and dreaming. On the court, his plans began to jell in 1959, but Ozzie Wadewitz would tell you that it really started to unfold in the fall of 1956, when a frightened eighth grade class came to high school for the very first time.

Pieces to the puzzle arrived with a variety of backgrounds and from different neighborhoods. Tommy Roberts went to Adair Elementary. Ozzie and Richard Wadewitz had seen him play Gra-Y basketball so his gifts were well known. Bob Tuggle, Virlyn Gaynes, Bart Hickman and Billy Seabrook were classmates at Sylvan Elementary. Lee DeFore and Ronnie Dodson were friends from Capitol View Elementary.

Terry Stephens was a totally new face. Stephens and his little brother were in foster care. They lived in Oak Hill Children's Home on Stewart Avenue so he attended Hutcheson Elementary School on Cleveland Avenue.

Most of this group was on Coach Steve Vernarsky's eighth grade basketball team. Stephens, because of his late April birthday, could not play for Vernarsky so he was advanced to the B-Team. DeFore did not even go out for the team that first year.

Familiar names started to show up in the B-Team scorebook the following season but a big one was still missing. DeFore, a gangly 6-foot-3, went out for the team but Coach Clem Knight sent the awkward freshman packing in his first round of cuts. That was not surprising, for though he looked like a basketball player, DeFore's only marketable skill was his height. That is what Wadewitz noticed later in PE class.

"Why aren't you playing basketball?" he asked.

"I got cut."

"If you want to play, I'll speak to Coach Knight," Wadewitz said.

Knight put DeFore back on the squad, but he never promised Wadewitz he would play him. DeFore did not see a minute of action for the B-Team that entire season but work had begun on the building of a basketball player.

Lee's father, Dick DeFore, acting on the advice of the varsity coach, put up a basketball goal on a pine tree in the backyard of their home in Capitol

View and the youngster started spending his spare time out there. Every day was the same. One shot with his left hand. One shot with his right. One shot with his left hand. One shot with his right. His shooting improved but there was much more to do before he would be a productive player.

"I thought if I worked hard that I'd make the B-Team that next year. But the first real basketball game I ever played in I was a starter on the varsity," DeFore relates.

Wadewitz was assembling his cast of characters. When practice began, the 1959 varsity team depended on the scoring of Doug Cooper, an All-State quarterback on the football team. Fellow senior John Hall provided a steady presence down low. But to the surprise of many, when the season began sophomores Roberts, Stephens and DeFore were in the lineup, leaving upper-classmen on the bench.

DeFore played but he did not look comfortable. He had 39 points in Sylvan's first seven games and scored in double figures twice. But as opponents exposed his weaknesses, he floundered. In the next 11 games, he tallied 13 points. For the season, he averaged a meager 2.9 points a game.

Down the stretch, fellow-sophomore Virlyn Gaynes was promoted from the B-Team and DeFore found himself on the bench more than he did on the court. When the coach did put the stumbling DeFore into a game, even loyal Sylvan fans booed.

"I knew what people were saying, but I kept working hard and Ozzie never gave up on me," DeFore says.

Gaynes took DeFore's starting spot late in the season and in the city tournament. He was several inches shorter than DeFore but his quickness and jumping ability made him effective on both ends of the court.

Gaynes' older brother, Charles, played for Wadewitz and his little brother attended most of the games. Basketball was Virlyn's dream. He was 6-foot-2 with long, basketball muscles but he desperately wanted to be taller. He finally set up a chinning bar in his backyard and would hang there for hours, hoping to add length.

In the city tournament, people started to notice the surprising Bears. Sylvan rolled over Bass in the first game and drew Murphy, the defending state champions, in the second round. It was a game in which Sylvan players began to believe in each other and their coach began to believe in himself.

Wadewitz's plan worked to perfection though the Eagles prevailed 56-53. The Golden Bears came up one game shy of a spot in the 1959 state tournament.

Sylvan finished 16-10 — the best record in school history. Two losses were to 1959 state champion Brown and one was to 1958 state champion Murphy. Those things were positives. Then again, there were the graduations of Hall and Cooper — an All-City performer and one of the state's scoring leaders. Teammates wished them well, but people close to the team were beginning to sense there was magic in the air.

And there was.

———

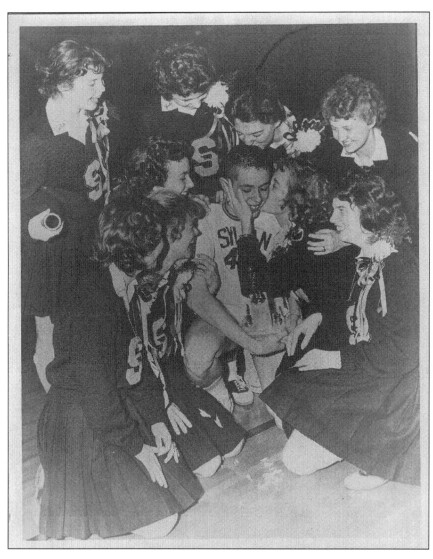

Cheerleaders swamp Tommy Roberts after he was named tournament MVP in 1960.

8

Ozzie's Crystal Ball

O zzie Wadewitz squeezed a small piece of chalk between the fingers of his left hand and in his illegible scrawl the veteran basketball coach scribbled something on top of his old wooden desk. Usually, he diagrammed plays, but something else was on his mind this time.

Wadewitz had been Billy Seabrook's homeroom teacher and B-Team football coach. The popular sophomore regularly visited the coach's offices underneath the gym so he felt at home. He does not remember now if he asked the coach what he was writing or whether Wadewitz volunteered it, but the message is still vivid.

"He wrote C-60, and when I asked him what that meant he said it stood for Championship 1960. 'We're going to win the state championship in 1960,' he said. Yeah, right, I thought. But he had the vision."

Most people would have reacted just like Seabrook did. After all, this was a high school that had never played a game in the state tournament. This was a team that won a school record 16 games in 1959, but it was a team that graduated its leading scorer and its most effective rebounder. It was a team that lacked personality, experience and leadership. But, of course, record books verify that Sylvan Hills High did win the state basketball title in 1960. And they repeated in 1961.

The quilt Wadewitz had been sewing was almost assembled. He could see this team had a future, but when a sports writer asked about his prospects, the coach was typically quiet. So when the season tipped off, the Golden Bears were playing under the radar.

Tommy Roberts was the only Sylvan player selected when the Atlanta newspapers published their pre-season all-city teams. On the court, Roberts was expected to pick up the scoring void left by Doug Cooper's departure. Terry Stephens, best known for his ball handling, was showing he could score too. Virlyn Gaynes was unorthodox but his innate jumping ability and hustle made up for his mistakes. Lee DeFore, overmatched as a sophomore, showed surprising confidence and potential.

The fifth spot was up for grabs. Early on, Lee Hammond — the only senior on the roster as play began — got some starts. So did juniors Ronnie Dodson and Bob Tuggle and sophomore Charles Robinson. Sophomore Charles Jordan, a bruiser from the football team, also got some minutes. Wadewitz was searching for the right ingredient and the right personnel.

A victory on Southwest's home court drew attention but Wadewitz said it was too early to brag. "We've been up and down and I don't think my boys have come into their own yet. We're a young club and we've played some good ball and bad ball this season. I just don't know what to expect next."

A 71-37 victory over George High set a school scoring record but Wadewitz's comment about the team's unpredictable nature came to mind when the Bears immediately dropped a 55-53 decision to Brown. At 9-3, Sylvan was the year's biggest surprise, according to sportswriter Gene Asher. He was impressed with the team's shooting but Wadewitz countered with a typical concern for its mistakes. "Until we correct those faults, we could shoot 50 percent and we still wouldn't win."

A SOLUTION WAS right there on the Sylvan bench. When Bob Tuggle was in the game, there was calmness. He was mentally tough, and it showed. He couldn't shoot as well as Roberts or DeFore, handle the ball like Stephens or leap like Gaynes but he knew where he was supposed to be and when he was supposed to be there. He knew his place and he knew his role.

"He was the fifth piece," Stephens says.

Wadewitz finally settled on his starting lineup but the team still had flaws, particularly on the boards. They lost their regular season finale to Brown by two and finished third in the city's Western Division with a record of 13-6. Ahead was the 3AAA tournament at Georgia Tech's Alexander Memorial Coliseum.

In 1959, the Bears surprised people but Sylvan almost got surprised in 1960. With Roberts, Stephens and Tuggle burdened with four fouls, Roosevelt was on its way to an upset until Roberts dropped in four late points to seal a 47-45 victory.

Up next was Murphy, defending city champs and the team that dashed Sylvan's hopes the previous year. Not this time. With Roberts scoring 15 of his 21 points in the first half, Sylvan recorded a convincing 59-40 victory. DeFore had 11, but more importantly pulled down 17 rebounds. That victory secured Sylvan High a spot in the State AAA basketball tournament for the first time in the 10-year history of the school.

Celebrating did not continue for long. It was time for another game with Brown. Unlike previous meetings, this one was not close. Sylvan thundered to earth with a thud, falling to Brown 56-38. All that was left was the consolation game with North Fulton. Playing for pride, the Bears settled for third in the city.

THE 1960 GEORGIA State AAA Tournament came at a time basketball was emerging from the shadows in Georgia. After years of discussing a facility on campus, Georgia Tech dedicated Alexander Memorial Coliseum on November 30, 1956. Earl Shell, a walk-on from Sylvan, played in the first game under the dome, starting in the backcourt opposite future U.S. Senator Sam Nunn in the freshman game. Coincidentally, when Tech's coliseum underwent its last major facelift in 1996, Shell's firm, Hardin Construction Company, handled the renovation work.

The tournament had moved to Tech from the old Atlanta City Auditorium in 1957. Less than a decade before, the title was decided at the Atlanta Sports Arena, a shoebox facility off Memorial Drive that was best known as a site for professional wrasslin' matches.

The event drew little interest and few fans until 1952 when the Georgia High School Athletic Association partnered with *The Atlanta Constitution* and moved games to the City Auditorium. The newspaper purchased a portable floor and the tournament became a winner on the court and at the turnstiles.

With the newspaper a partner in the tournament, coverage of high school basketball increased. At the same time, Georgia Tech evolved into a contender in the SEC. Wins over Kentucky made headlines and tiny guards Buddy Blemker and Terry Randall sparked some entertaining teams when the Jackets moved into the coliseum.

But the true headline maker was Roger Kaiser — Tech's only two-time All-American. As a sophomore, he played out of position with Blemker and Randall but he crashed the national scene in 1959 by teaming with flashy Dave Denton to take Tech to the NCAA Tournament for the first time. He was even better in 1960, finishing with 18 of Tech's 25 school records.

Sylvan would be playing on the court where Kaiser was king. The Bears had played there in region games but this was the state tournament. Tommy Roberts says the Bears were not intimidated as they prepared to play perennial power Baker High of Columbus.

During Sylvan's amazing title run in 1960, juniors Virlyn Gaynes, Bob Tuggle, Lee DeFore, Tommy Roberts and Terry Stephens were Coach Ozzie Wadewitz' iron men.

"That was Ozzie's doing," he says. "We were very confident. I don't remember being afraid at all."

There was no fear but was there confidence?

DeFore looks back with candor: "We were just trying to make it to the state tournament. Our region was pretty tough. The last two state champions came out of Atlanta. We knew if you came out of that region you had a good chance. We wanted to get there and play well."

Not everyone agreed with that assessment and some said so in print. Throughout the tournament, Charlie Roberts of The Constitution and Gene

Asher of The Journal picked Sylvan to lose. The Bears were, after all, a team without a senior and a school that had never been there before.

Preparing for the tournament, Wadewitz called Charlie Aldridge, the head coach at Russell High in East Point. Russell's gym had glass backboards and Wadewitz wanted his team to get used to them before tournament play. He was trying to take away any doubts in the minds of his young team.

Wadewitz found out a lot in the opener against 19-4 Baker. Coach Bubba Ball won state titles in 1954 and 1956. The Lions were on their way to another in 1955 but lost in the state semi-finals to Columbus High — an in-town rival that the Lions had dominated back home.

Ball's teams ran the "shuffle," an intricate offense that befuddled many opponents. Sylvan was not one of them. Experts had predicted Baker and LaGrange were the down state contenders to win it all along with Brown. Only they were wrong.

Sylvan, in its first state tournament appearance, sent Baker back to Columbus with bitter memories of a 40-37 upset. Showing that was not a fluke, the Bears came back the next night to upend Campbell-Smyrna 41-38.

Like Baker and Columbus in 1955, Brown figured they owned the Golden Bears. They had defeated them three times in city play and now they were facing them for the second time in a week on the floor at Tech — this time in the state semi-finals.

The match-up was huge to Bob Tuggle. He moved to Sylvan Road in the fifth grade. Prior to that he lived on Beecher Street, a jump shot away from Brown High. "My best friend from the time I was 5 until I was 10 was Eddie Jordan. He played for Brown and as juniors they won the state championship. In 1960, they beat us three times before we played them in the state."

Tuggle scored 15 points and Sylvan won the game that counted as the Bears shocked the Rebels 57-45 to advance to the state finals against LaGrange, a team that had lost only one game prior to the trip to Atlanta.

The Grangers featured Donnie Mahaffey, a member of a basketball family that kept Clemson University stocked in players for more than a decade. The family had four sons: Tom, Don, Randy and Richie. Each stood around 6-foot-7 and each one was dominating on the boards. Sharp-shooting Jerry Smith joined Donnie in the Grangers lineup. Against Northside of Atlanta the night before, Smith tossed in 31 points from long range.

"Ozzie had scouted them before. He knew what it took for Smith to get his shot. He put in a special defense about an hour before the game and we shut Smith down completely," recalls Terry Stephens, the man that chased the LaGrange star all night.

More than strategy was going on in the Sylvan locker room. Tommy Roberts somehow arrived at the coliseum without his game shorts. Lanky freshman Steve Copeland knew he was the obvious choice to give up his shorts so he left the room. This was a big night for him. He grew up in LaGrange and came to Sylvan in the 8th grade. He looked forward to seeing former classmates.

Larry Bell, a student manager, finally found the vanishing Copeland and said the coach wanted to see him. "Roberts has forgotten his black game shorts. You need to give him yours," Wadewitz said.

"What am I going to wear?" Copeland answered.

"Brown is playing in the consolation game. When they come back up here, see if one of them will let you wear a pair of their shorts," the coach said.

Copeland knew there was nothing more to say so he took off his shorts and stood there in his jersey, jockey strap, socks and shoes. That was what he was wearing when the Brown team came back to their assigned dressing room.

Buddy King saw the half-naked Sylvan player first.

"What are you doing, Copeland?" he laughed.

"Roberts forgot his shorts and I gave him mine. I need a pair of shorts to wear."

King didn't hesitate.

"He took off his old sweaty blue and gray shorts and handed them to me. I didn't say a word. I just put them on and headed for the tunnel. It had only been a little over a year since I went to school with just about everybody on the LaGrange team. My mother worked for Mr. Mahaffey at the mill for 25 years. They stopped their warm-ups and laughed at me."

Copeland laughed last.

"My shorts won the MVP," he says.

Experts were no longer experts. Sylvan High upended LaGrange 49-42 to become the 1960 Georgia AAA State Basketball Champions. Roberts — wearing Copeland's shorts — was voted the tournament's Most Valuable Player. The Golden Bears ran the table without making a substitution. Roberts, DeFore,

Stephens, Gaynes and Tuggle played every minute and every minute they wore rubber bands on their wrists that Tuggle suggested they wear for luck.

FANS WERE OVERJOYED. This was a night they had waited on for ten years. They had been upset all week as writers predicted Sylvan's downfall every day. In the end, that made the championship sweeter. But when Constitution sports editor Jesse Outlar and prep writer Charlie Roberts went to courtside to participate in the ceremony, Sylvan folks offered playful boos.

When the ceremony began, student manager Bill England quietly gathered his belongings. Throughout the season, he sat at the scorer's table but that was not allowed at the state level. He and fellow manager Ronnie Pipkin had to sit on the bench. Someone told England that team managers were always thrown into the showers after winning a state title and England intended to stay dry.

As officials from the Georgia High School Association and The Constitution presented the awards, England and Pipkin sneaked up the tunnel to the Sylvan locker room. "Ronnie and I got undressed, hid our clothes and were in the showers when the team finally got there," England laughs.

The Bears, 20-8, were the champions of Georgia but when they shed their uniforms they were teen-agers again. It was too late for a party but the players wanted to stay together so they could absorb all that happened together. They decided to meet at Virlyn Gaynes' house.

DeFore paints a picture of the impromptu celebration: "We sat around the living room at Virlyn's house and laughed and talked all night. When it got time to sleep some of us were on pillows on the floor, some spread out on the sofa and some were in chairs. We didn't do much sleeping, really. Around 4 a.m., we piled into somebody's car and drove to downtown Atlanta. We found a newspaper box and bought early editions of Sunday's Journal-Constitution so we could see what they wrote about the 'Cinderella Team.'"

On the front of the sports page was Charlie Roberts' game story. Attached to it was a mug shot of Roberts, wearing his signature Fedora. He was a familiar face around high school games for decades. His colorful style was well known and he kept alive the Cinderella theme in his Sunday story.

The Alexander Memorial Coliseum clock never struck 12 for Sylvan High's five Cinderella Kids. It never will. For Saturday night, playing before a packed Round House that included 5,465 paying customers, the unsung, un-feared and underrated Golden Bears smote down favored LaGrange, 49-42, in the finals of the Georgia High School Association's Constitution sponsored State Class AAA bas-ketball tournament.

Monday morning frazzled members of Cinderella's favorite team were back in class at Sylvan High. Only learning would have to wait. Everywhere they went — in class, in the halls and in the cafeteria — they were singled out. They were heroes and they were champions. But as raucous cheers from Saturday night still rang in their ears, people started wondering if the Golden Bears could do it again next year.

It was a question that would not go away.

———

FORTIETH

Georgia High School Association

State Basketball Tournament

Class AAA -- Boys

Alexander Memorial Coliseum — Georgia Tech — Atlanta

March 1, 2, 3, 4, 1961

Sessions:

Session 1 — Wednesday .... 10:30 A. M., 12, 1:30, 3, 4:30, 6, 7:30, 9 P. M.
Session 2 — Thursday .... 4:30, 6, 7:30, 9 P. M.
Session 3 — Friday .... 7:30, 9 P. M.
Session 4 — Saturday .... 7, 8:30 P. M.

Tournament Officials

Referees: Arnold Satterfield, T. W. Robinson, Jimmy Johnson, Fred Caswell
Timers: Joe Sieracki, Joe Kennedy
Scorers: John Nance, Clyde Partin
Honorary Scorer: Roy White
Announcer: Roy T. Hartsfield
Business Manager: George O'Kelly

Previous Winners

1922	Lanier	1935	Tech High	1948	Lanier
1923	Boys High	1936	Lanier	1949	Roosevelt
1924	U. S. B.	1937	Savannah	1950	Lanier
1925	Lanier	1938	Lanier	1951	Lanier
1926	Lanier	1939	Lanier	1952	Brown
1927	Lanier	1940	Lanier	1953	North Fulton
1928	Lanier	1941	Savannah	1954	Baker
1929	Tech High	1942	Lanier	1955	Russell
1930	Savannah	1943	Jordan	1956	Baker
1031	Savannah	1944	Columbus	1957	Decatur
1932	Savannah	1945	Lanier	1958	Murphy
1933	Lanier	1946	Savannah	1959	Brown
1934	Lanier	1947	Savannah	1960	Sylvan
				1961	Sylvan

9

Almost Perfect

O
n the eve of the 40th state high school basketball tournament, *Atlanta Constitution* sports editor Jesse Outlar wrote about the anticipated return of Sylvan High School's defending champions and other teams that would be focusing on Ozzie Wadewitz's Golden Bears.

"It's Sylvan against the world," Outlar wrote.

The veteran sports columnist referred to teams that would be competing at Alexander Memorial Coliseum that coming week. Outlar did not stop to consider that Sylvan had been playing against the world for almost a year.

With a lineup of juniors that never sat down, the Bears shocked opponents and supporters alike by taking the 1960 title back to a school that had never celebrated a state championship before. They came in the back door of the coliseum and nobody noticed. Twelve months later, with just one unusual loss held against them, the Bears returned with flash bulbs popping and expectations flapping from the rafters of Tech's dome.

The 1961 season was hardly underway before writers noted the challenges they faced. No basketball team in Georgia had won two state titles in a row since Coach Selby Buck and Lanier of Macon in 1951. Baker of Columbus won the trophy in 1954, and came back unbeaten in 1955, only to lose to Columbus

High, their hometown rivals. As a reminder how tough a repeat was, Baker came back to win the 1956 championship. Murphy and Brown had young teams but could not repeat. It was a monologue Wadewitz tired of hearing.

No one had to remind Sylvan players how tough it would be to repeat. They were nothing more than high school kids, but the 1960 tournament seasoned them. Every day they opened the Atlanta newspapers and read someone predicting their downfall. In their presence, they heard their faults and flaws discussed by grownup coaches that should have known better. These events brought them closer as a team and that closeness made them stronger.

"We genuinely liked each other. This is the intangible that elevates a very good team to greatness," says Lee DeFore — an individual that elevated himself to greatness between those two seasons.

But man cannot live on intangibles alone. He must have work and before the championship trophy had time to gather dust Sylvan players were lacing up their shoes again. Putting their growing press clippings aside, they hurried back to the basketball court.

"If we weren't practicing, we were playing somewhere else," Terry Stephens says. "We just liked to play."

WHETHER SCHOOL WAS in session or not, Wadewitz made sure they had a place to play. The window by the back entrance to the locker rooms at the Sylvan gym was inexplicably left unlocked most weekends and the fellows showed up one by one. There were no cheering fans in the bleachers and no referees on the court but most Saturdays and Sundays there were ten guys running up and down the court.

Wadewitz had been installing a full-court press. The Bears used it some late in the 1959 season and showed it about half the time on their championship run the following year. The coach planned to use it all the time in 1961 and everyone realized how important depth would be.

During the off-season, some important new faces were added. Ronnie Dodson, Billy Seabrook and Charles Robinson were back from the title team though Charles Jordan decided to concentrate on football. New faces were now on the roster, and they would be important in 1961. Senior Bart Hickman was showing he could be a valuable back up at several positions. Sophomore Steve Copeland was gifted in basketball, football, track and baseball. At 6-foot-7 he could give DeFore needed rest. Jerry Baker, another promising sophomore, was already exhibiting unusual offensive skills. Wilson Culbreath, though he would likely end up on the B-Team, was ready if needed.

Later in the summer, the starting five of DeFore, Gaynes, Roberts, Stephens and Tuggle attended a basketball camp conducted by Coach Garland Pinholster at Oglethorpe University. The Sylvan five was joined by high school players from Marist, Druid Hills and Campbell-Smyrna — a team the Bears would get to know much better down the road.

It was an education for DeFore: "Most of those teams were returning most of their starters from the year before. At that point, we realized we had a chemistry that the other teams didn't have. We had some bloody battles — literally — that summer and we won all of them."

Once school started in September, the Georgia High School Athletic Association set limits on practice time — particularly if the coach was present. Some of the players attended Capitol View Baptist Church and had spent a lot of time in the church gym. Bobby Ward — a 1952 Sylvan graduate — became friends with Wadewitz after being cut from the first Golden Bear team. He invited the team to work out at Capitol View.

"They would set up a time and when they showed up there was always a game going on. They would just play and play and play. They would stay as long as I let them," says Ward, later head basketball coach and athletic director at Westminster Schools in Atlanta.

After-school vigils at Capitol View improved their basketball skills and conditioning and were also important to team unity. DeFore remembers those afternoons: "Roberts, Copeland and Seabrook were playing football but the rest of us would put on our trunks, gather up some basketballs and head for the church. We dribbled along Dill Avenue and then we had a little cutover that we took to the gym. All of it was fun."

THEIR COACH WAS also at work. Ozzie and Dick Wadewitz — as they always did in the off-season — compared notes. "We would talk about what worked and what didn't," Dick says. "We used the same offense and same defense and we both started using the full-court press about the same time."

Dick spent four years as his older brother's assistant at Sylvan before returning to Wisconsin to be head coach at Lincoln High School in Milwaukee. The year before Ozzie's first state title in Georgia, Dick's team won the 1959 championship in Wisconsin. Lincoln won again in 1961 and 1962 and during one stretch, racked up 49 victories in a row. In 1963, Dick moved into the college ranks as an assistant at the University of Wisconsin-Plattsville and became head coach a year later. He stayed there 20 years, took the team to several NCAA tournaments and is in the UWP Hall of Fame.

His brother's success at Milwaukee-Lincoln only added to Ozzie Wadewitz's drive to win that second state title in Georgia. He was also miffed at constant reminders from the press about how many teams in Georgia had failed to repeat. But most of the pressure on the unassuming coach came from within, pressures that began on that makeshift basketball court in the building behind his father's butcher shop in Slinger.

Special teams mean special challenges. Wadewitz had to guard against over confidence and cockiness. He knew the team had to get better and not stagnate. He had to make sure they were ready to play every night they went on the court because opponents would always be ready to play the defending state champs.

Five starters were back but there were still personnel questions. Wadewitz had an established player in Roberts and an emerging star in DeFore. Having two offensive threats often means one of the players feels he does not get the ball enough, which leads to pouting. Wadewitz also recognized that the frenetic style he was adopting on defense and offense would mean a different rotation and more minutes for the fellows on the bench. They were a family but even families can have issues.

Terry Stephens was part of that family and he has never forgotten what his teammates' acceptance meant to him as a player and as a human being. He had been in and out of foster care most of his childhood and lived in Oak Hill Children's Home, near the drive-in theater on Stewart Avenue when he started to Sylvan. Basketball and baseball were his escapes. In Wadewitz he found a father figure and in his teammates he found a family.

"I didn't have any money and I didn't have a car. But from the time I started playing with those guys it was like I had 10 or 12 brothers. When somebody made plans, I didn't have to say a word. Someone would say, 'I'll go pick up Terry.' They let me know I belonged," Stephens says.

Behind the scenes, bureaucracy and child services got in Stephens' way. His date of birth was an issue and with the opening of Walter F. George, residents of Oak Hill were being reassigned to the new high school. Wadewitz and Sylvan principal James C. Fain intervened. Basketball was only part of their concern. They knew how important the team had become to the young man and his wellbeing.

Fain filed a hardship request asking that Stephens be allowed to remain at Sylvan. While that was pending, he moved in with the Abernathy family. Ray, George and Carol were his classmates and their parents had provided a home to foster children for many years. "I could have gone back to Oak Hill and still gone to Sylvan but the Abernathys became my family," Stephens says. "Through the years, they have always been there for me."

DeFore was undergoing changes of another kind. When he first suited up in the ninth grade, he was a plundering, overgrown kid. As a sophomore, he struggled. As a junior, he showed potential.

During the summer before his senior year, he came into his own. Physically, he grew an inch and a half and he added 20 pounds. As a basketball player, the hours he spent alone in the gym and the time he sacrificed shooting at that basket on the tree in his backyard were beginning to show.

Roberts was in a quandary most athletes would welcome. Major college football coaches were interested in him as a quarterback and their counterparts in basketball were telling Roberts to stick to hoops. He was one of those unusual athletes that had the natural ability to excel at either sport in college. The MVP of the 1960 state tournament was the only member of Sylvan's starting five still playing football in 1961 since Tuggle had given up the sport to prepare for basketball.

OBSERVERS NATURALLY TALKED about the team's returning starters as the 1961 season drew near. Wadewitz, meanwhile, had to make sure egos were checked at the door. He did that by instigating a rigorous practice routine that kept the whole team on their toes — even the headliners.

A practice ladder was established and every day players competed in shooting, free throws, layups and other key categories. Even the reserves had the right to challenge anyone above them on the ladder in a given category — including the starters. No one wanted to see their name at the bottom rung.

Practice was run on the clock — 10 minutes for this and 20 minutes for that. "Ozzie was as organized as anybody I've ever come in contact with," Roberts says. "He didn't waste a lot of time."

Ozzie Wadewitz had faith in Lee DeFore when others did not.

But the moment of truth every day came when it was time to scrimmage. It wasn't show time. This was a reality show and a gut check. Pride was on the line. So were extra laps. On one team was DeFore, Gaynes, Roberts, Stephens and Tuggle. On the other was a combination of Dodson, Seabrook, Robinson, Hickman, Baker and Copeland. The scoreboard was turned on and every scrimmage began with the second team being spotted a six, eight or even a 10-point lead.

"As part of his madness, the first team had to play from behind every single day," Baker says. "That paid off several times during the season."

The competitive edge and confidence this gave members of the second unit also paid off. If a starter got into foul trouble or was ill, someone off the bench was ready.

"We had the best second five in the state," DeFore says flatly. "Dodson could have been a star anywhere else. Charles Robinson, Bart Hickman, Billy Seabrook, Steve Copeland and Jerry Baker made us work hard every day. I think they were as good or better than most teams we played. When it was game time, we had been challenged every day in practice."

The team's fast break would be eye catching but Wadewitz added a wrinkle in the Bears' half-court offense that never failed. The play was called "Dog Gone" — as in DeFore and Gaynes. A pick was set for a DeFore jump shot and if the defense overreacted Gaynes slashed to the basket. It was used mainly in the third quarter and was designed to help put a game away. Wadewitz called it 30 times that season and 30 times it produced points.

Another ploy made more noise. Though Wadewitz maintained a business-like approach, one thing his team did every night was all show biz — and it may have been worth 10 points on the scoreboard. When Sylvan first emerged from the dressing room, they warmed up in a typical fashion. When those exercises were done, a message was sent that was not lost on opposing huddles.

"We'd come back out and slam it," Baker says.

Everyone recognized Gaynes's ability to sky. DeFore had grown to 6-foot-7 and Tuggle was 6-foot-4. What people forgot was that Copeland and Seabrook were high jumpers on the track team so they could also get off the floor. Seven out of the 10 guys on the Sylvan bench could dunk and opponents had to notice. The dunk may not have been a legal weapon at that time but it made an impression right before the opening whistle.

Fans might not have picked up this subtle nuance but the Sylvan faithful could not wait for the season to formally tip off. Cheering for a state championship team was a new experience. Though the school opened in 1950, basketball was a team without a home during its first four seasons. The Bears were nomads, practicing and playing all over town, making it difficult for fans as well as players. Attendance at home had been growing since Earl Shell and friends made it to the city finals in 1956, and it mushroomed during the first title run in 1960.

Football continued to rule but that was changing. The Golden Bear football team had shown promise but faces were long after disappointing records of 5-5 and 4-6 — despite a roster filled with talent and potential. Going into the 1961 season, Sylvan was picked to win the city title in football only to finish with a losing record. That added to the anticipation of watching Ozzie's boys defend their championship.

The basketball season opened November 19 with a non-region victory at Grady High. Two nights later, in their first home game, the Bears defeated Roosevelt. The third game was the strangest outing of the season. Playing at home, a storm left the gym in darkness and the game had to be called in the second quarter. It went into the books as a 29-17 victory over North Fulton. A win is a win but those numbers have forever haunted team and individual stats.

Sylvan ended its non-region schedule with rousing victories over Murphy and East Atlanta. Early games were only warm-ups for what was ahead. In the region opener, Sylvan blistered Dykes 75-36. Or, as The Constitution's Charlie Roberts put it: "Sylvan High's championship special zoomed off the launching pad on schedule and rocketed to a stratospheric shattering of the Dykes Colts." As a harbinger of things to come, DeFore had 17 points by halftime and then joined the other starters as spectators as the second unit went the rest of the way. Dodson had 12, Baker 9, Robinson 5, Seabrook 4 and Hickman 4.

The following night, Sylvan traveled across town to face Northside — a team that Wadewitz had never beaten. The Tigers were billed as challengers in the region but the Bears rolled to a 74-57 victory. DeFore poured in 28 points. Roberts finished with 12 and Gaynes added 11. Once again, the bench was vital as three starters fouled out.

MONTHS BEFORE, THE Atlanta Tip-Off Club and *Atlanta Journal* sportswriter Gene Asher had arranged holiday doubleheaders featuring Sylvan and Campbell of Smyrna against two ranked teams from the basketball-rich Commonwealth of Kentucky. Newport, No. 11 in Kentucky, and third-ranked Ashland would play two nights of basketball while they were in Atlanta. In a twist of irony, the two Georgia teams would meet again the following March in the state AAA championship game.

Pundits saw the games as measuring sticks for prep basketball in Georgia. The game had taken great strides and the contention was that the best teams in Georgia could now compete with teams from anywhere — even Kentucky and Indiana. Previews of the games started appearing in the Journal and the Constitution weeks before the contests. At Sylvan, where the Bears would be the host team both nights, extra bleachers were secured and placed behind the basket at one end of the court.

The Bears, 8-0 against local competition, defeated Newport 64-58 in a struggle where the lead changed hands 10 times in the last 12 minutes. DeFore had 32 and Tuggle had 11. Up the road in Cobb County, Ashland took care of business with a 64-48 victory over Campbell of Smyrna.

Campbell of Smyrna saved face with a 64-63 win over Newport in the Saturday opener at Sylvan. The main event spotlighted Ashland and Sylvan — teams that would be the 1961 state champions of Kentucky and Georgia.

Fans who marveled at Sylvan's relentless pressing defense and fast-break offense were in shock as Ashland raced to an 87-68 victory on the Golden Bears' home floor. Sportswriter Tom Stoddard said the visitors "harassing Sylvan unmercifully on defense and pouring in more than enough field goals from near and far, ran, ran, ran, to a win."

Decades later, that game can be put in perspective. A newspaper poll in the Blue Grass state in 2011 rated Ashland the best high school basketball team in the history of Kentucky. That same season, the Tomcats, 36-1, also beat Portsmouth, the state champions of Ohio.

All five Ashland starters played major college basketball. Larry Conley, now a busy TV commentator, was a three-year starter at Kentucky and was All-SEC in 1966. Harold Sergeant, who scored 31 against Sylvan, starred at Morehead State and was named to the all-Ohio Valley Conference team three years in a row.

An article in a Kentucky newspaper after the 50th anniversary of that Ashland team was celebrated at Rupp Arena in Lexington claimed Sylvan assumed they would manhandle the Tom Cats. DeFore says that is not so.

"We certainly didn't think we were going to lay it on them … That was early in the season. We hadn't hit our stride and I know I hadn't hit my own stride. I wish we could have played them later in the year."

In *Teamwork*, a 2011 book on the Ashland team, author Mark Maynard quotes former Louisville Courier-Journal sports editor Billy Reed who said the Tom Cats played the game the way it should be played. "Today, so much emphasis is on individual talent and sheer athleticism, rather than team accomplishments. There's a lot of beauty to the game, the team aspects of it, that seem to be forgotten. That team played the game so well together and were so unselfish … Everybody made a contribution in different ways. Individually they all had special things they did. Collectively they were the epitome of team."

Ashland went home with the respect of the Sylvan team. They also left with friendships, as DeFore rediscovered after the death of his mother. Going through her things, he found stacks of letters he exchanged with Sergeant, the sharp-shooting Ashland guard. "There were no emails or cell phones but we kept in touch. Some Ashland guys even stopped that year on their way to Florida."

Though the Bears certainly wished the final score of that game with Ashland had been different, they were undaunted. In many ways, that loss stings more today than it did then. They so wish they could look back on a totally unblemished season. But Wadewitz did not let them stay down. He used the loss as a teaching tool, vowing that no other team would successfully use a pressing defense against them again. It was something he mentioned every day in practice.

THE BEARS RETURNED to the court with a vengeance. They destroyed George 94-38 and a week later, with subs playing most of the way, defeated Therrell 116-35 — setting a new city team scoring record. DeFore stayed around long enough to tally 25 points. Tuggle and Roberts had 10 each. But the bench did most of the damage, racking up 58 points of their own. Dodson had 18. Seabrook and Baker had 15 each. Sophomore Baker put them over the century mark with less than five minutes to play.

Paul Atkinson of The Constitution watched Sylvan dismantle Therrell. Afterward, he talked to Wadewitz about the loss to Ashland and the easy win over outmanned Therrell — a team that should have been playing a B-Team schedule. "One thing we learned against Ashland: We are not invincible," the

Sylvan coach said. "The dice are loaded against us this time more than ever ... However let me say this. I credit these kids of mine with being level-headed enough, so that if they lose, it won't be because of overconfidence."

No one knew it then, but the Bears march to the state tournament had begun. They traveled to East Point to pick up the first place trophy in the third annual Metropolitan Tournament and the margins of victory down the stretch tell an amazing story. On its way to the city tournament, Sylvan defeated George by 44, Russell by 30, Marietta by 15, Smith by 29, West Fulton by 31, Southwest by 35, O'Keefe by 19, Brown by 32, Dykes by 38, Northside by 3, George by 18, Therrell by 66, West Fulton 27, Southwest by 20, O'Keefe by 36 and Brown by 28.

They did this despite Tuggle missing two weeks with a glandular problem and Stephens missing action with an injured shoulder. Tuggle showed he was recovered by scoring a career high 18 points against his childhood neighbors from Brown in Sylvan's final game at home. Down the stretch, Roberts rekindled his shooting touch and DeFore continued his torrid pace. He topped the city in scoring and fought off future Auburn University teammate Freddie Guy of Avondale for the lead statewide.

Before the state tournament there was other business. Sylvan had never won a city championship and the Bears wanted to add this piece of gold to their trophy case. In the opener, East Atlanta fell 69-41 with DeFore and Stephens scoring 19 apiece. This set up a fourth game with Walter F. George. In the previous meeting, the Falcons put on a show, losing a 91-73 shootout with Sylvan transfers Steve Davis, Richard Lovvern and W.B. Norton scoring 32, 18 and 8 respectively.

Before the game in the city tournament, George head coach Pat Stephens talked about the Bears. "We are not scared of Sylvan," he said, "but we may as well face it. Those guys are not human."

He was right. The Bears rolled to an 82-52 win. DeFore led with 26 followed by Tuggle with 14. Davis, an All-City selection, was held to six, as was Norton. Lovvorn led George with 10.

The following night, Sylvan hit 52 percent of their field goal attempts and defeated defensive-minded North Fulton 83-57. Roberts, feeling at home at Tech's Alexander Memorial Coliseum, led the attack with 28 followed by DeFore with 18 and Stephens with 14.

Their opponent in the title game was Murphy, a team the Bears defeated by 13 early in the season. Describing what happened, Gene Asher wrote: "The Sylvan High basketball team is like a delayed bomb. You never know when it will explode." Against the Eagles, it exploded in the second half as the Bears won the school's first city title with a commanding 67-36 victory over Murphy. DeFore was the scoring leader with 24, Roberts had 15 and Tuggle 10.

Directly ahead was the state tournament and the Bears were the prohibitive favorite. Wadewitz accepted that and talked about his squad's 36-game winning streak against Georgia teams. "I don't like being the favorite but there's nothing I can do about it. I'd certainly rather be a 36-game winner than a 36-game loser. And I think the streak works in our favor, rather than against us. It not only gives the boys self-confidence, but every time we win it makes an impression on our next opponent. The pressure is on the teams that have to play us. After all, we're the champions."

CHAMPIONS, YES. BUT could they repeat? That question bounced through Tech's coliseum like a runaway beach ball as the tournament began. Like a vinyl record stuck in one groove, writer after writer discussed how]]favored teams had fallen in the past. But in Sylvan's opener with Richmond Academy, the Augusta quintet was put to sleep early. DeFore scored 18 points, followed by Gaynes with 14. Roberts and Stephens each had 12.

Second round action was billed a duel between DeFore and Avondale's Freddie Guy. All season long, they battled for the state scoring title, an honor eventually won by the Sylvan star's 24.5 average. Head-to-head, DeFore had 30 and Guy had 19 as the Bears held off Avondale 63-56. Tuggle's only bucket of the game put Sylvan up by five with four minutes to play.

Atlanta Journal sports writer Bill Robinson talked to DeFore after the victory and asked him, of all things, about his feet: "I've got the worst feet this side of the Abominable Snowman," DeFore laughed. But his teammates were no laughing matter. "We've come a long way together and we've had fun," he said, wistfully. "I hate to see this gang break up."

Two foes were in Sylvan's way and DeFore said it would not be easy. "We're in for a tough time. The Avondale game was the toughest game we've had since Ashland taught us we still had a lot to learn. We'll be lucky to get through to the finals."

The semi-finals reprised Sylvan's opener when Sylvan defeated cross-town rival Grady 72-48. Stakes were higher but the margin was about the same as the Bears earned a spot in the finals with a 64-41 win. Balance was the key as DeFore had 20, Roberts had 18 and Gaynes had 14.

Veteran Atlanta Constitution sports editor Jesse Outlar became a fan of Coach Ozzie Wadewitz's Golden Bears.

Jesse Outlar had seen enough. The finals were yet to be played, but in The Constitution he wrote that Sylvan was the best Georgia high school team he had ever seen.

> Ozzie Wadewitz's men may hit a cold streak and falter, but
> they deserve the roaring applause afforded them ... Personally,
> Sylvan has the best prep team I've seen in the state. Wade-
> witz has the horses, and he knows what to do with them.
> Sylvan is a superbly drilled team. The Golden Bears know
> what they are supposed to do, and they do it. Then, too, they
> are perhaps the best-conditioned outfit in the meet. They
> literally run contenders out of contention ... Even if they fail
> to retain the crown, Wadewitz's boys must be entered in the
> books with the best in Georgia's basketball annals.

A year of talking about whether Sylvan would repeat came down to one game.
The previous season, they defeated Campbell of Smyrna on their way to their
first title. Now the Bears and the Panthers were the last teams standing in 1961.

Looking on were 7,180 payees — the largest crowd to ever watch a basketball game in the state of Georgia, capping off a tournament that drew a record
26,082 paying customers. Thousands were turned away that night, including
Rosemary Wadewitz, the wife of the Sylvan coach. She drove around town and
listened to action on the radio. Like others, she missed seeing her husband's
team make history with a 62-58 win over Campbell of Smyrna.

As they did the year before, Sylvan's starting five went the distance. Roberts
led the victors with 19 points, but the 1960 MVP watched as DeFore, his
high-scoring teammate, won the outstanding player award for 1961. He was
also the leading scorer in the tournament.

DeFore took home the gold but Roberts broke the game wide open with
two driving layups at the start of the third period. Stephens followed with a
one-hander that put the Bears in total control and he also held sharpshooter
Jimmy Pitts to just three field goals. It was Pitts' final game in high school
before he embarked on an outstanding career at the University of Georgia.
Sylvan closed its remarkable year with a record of 36-1, going 54-8 in their
two championship seasons.

NO ONE WOULD have imagined it, but Sylvan's titles signaled the end of the
city's dominance in basketball. Roosevelt won in 1949. Brown won in 1952
and 1959. North Fulton was champion in 1953 and Murphy took the title in
1958. After Sylvan in 1960 and 1961, it was eight years before Carver-Atlanta

won the Class AA title. The balance of power shifted outside of the city and everything changed in 1967 with the desegregation of post-season events.

Neither the past nor the future mattered as Sylvan players finished the ceremonial side of the event. They had accomplished what they set out to do the preceding March. They were champions of Georgia, though it would be years before they truly understood the magnitude of it all.

"Coach told us that last night that we had done something people will never forget and will talk about forever. It was more than the starting five. It was a team of 12," Stephens says.

As sophomores, Baker and Copeland caught a ride on a magic carpet. But as Stephens noted, this was a team of 12 so substitutes had important parts to play. The Bears topped the 100-point barrier twice that season and both times Baker had the honor. Wadewitz also made sure he had a chance to score a basket at Alexander Memorial Coliseum.

Baker remembers when he first saw his name on the varsity roster. He was told to go pick up his uniform. "I went down to the equipment room and Tommy Roberts handed me my uniform. He had been the MVP at the state tournament the year before and he was handing ME my uniform. Wow!"

Baker calls that first unit a machine.

"We knew that better than anybody. We had to guard those guys every day. We finished up just about every game. Think what their stats would have been if they played all the way."

Tuggle received fewer headlines than anyone in the lineup. Others were stars. He was the role player. But at crucial moments in crucial games, there was Tuggle. To his teammates, he was the piece of the puzzle that had been missing. But to him, the secret ingredient was not a secret at all.

"We had the best basketball coach in the state of Georgia," he says. "He made us a championship team and he was such a wonderful influence on our lives. We had no concept what being on that team would be to our lives."

Bobby Ward was close to the players and a close friend of the coach. Looking back at that squad, he praises its unity. "They were a Band of Brothers. They played together for so long that they didn't just play as a team. They liked each other and they looked after each other. Talent isn't enough. They were a family."

Fans already looked ahead to 1962. Charles Robinson would be back and teammates said that in practice he was a better shooter than DeFore or Roberts.

Baker was an outside threat and at 6-foot-7 Copeland could be a dominant inside force. Wilson Culbreath gained experience on the B-Team and other players waited in the wings. No one dared mention another championship but everyone agreed Wadewitz would have talent that next season.

Or would he?

A FILM HAD been taken of the state championship game and Wadewitz wanted to share it with his players. Such a project was unique and expensive in those years and no one is sure who did the filming. The camera had been positioned high above Alexander Memorial Coliseum making players on the floor look like ants. No one complained though. This was a chance to celebrate one more time.

The coach borrowed a projector from the school and everyone gathered at Virlyn Gaynes' house in late April for the premiere showing of the grainy movie. After they watched it, Wadewitz said he had something important to tell them.

The news shocked everyone in the room, just as it would everyone at the school and around the city. Wadewitz — Georgia's reigning Coach of the Year — was leaving Sylvan High after 12 years to become head basketball coach at Wauwatosa East High School in Milwaukee, less than an hour from his hometown of Slinger.

Richard Wadewitz, his brother and former Sylvan assistant, was head basketball coach at Lincoln High in Milwaukee where he won state titles in 1959, 1961 and 1962. Wauwatosa East and Lincoln were in different regions but the chance to meet in the post-season was there.

"He said his brother Dick kind of talked him into it but that coaching at home was something he had always thought about," DeFore says, describing what happened that day. "I was shocked. I thought they had a chance to be pretty good that next year."

For the seniors, it was sad. For returning players, it was devastating. They were one victory away from a record for consecutive wins in Georgia and they assumed Ozzie would be their coach. They were teenagers, but they knew their world would not be the same without him.

As the news spread, reactions were similar.

"This is the worst news I've ever had. This will be a big blow to a lot of people," Sylvan Athletic Director Jack Wood said.

Citywide AD Sid Scarborough said no one should blame him since the move would better him financially. "We are sure the people of Milwaukee will be more than pleased with him. He is a fine Christian gentleman, in addition to being a fine teacher and coach."

Sylvan supporters were bewildered by Wadewitz's decision. He had been a vital part of the Golden Bear family since classes began in 1950. The joy and pride his championship teams had brought to the high school and to that part of town were immeasurable.

Right or wrong, residents of the south side had always felt they were treated as second-class citizens by the city at-large. But the success of those two basketball seasons had — for just a moment — given them an opportunity to brag and gloat about a neighborhood and a school that they loved so much. Those past two years had broken down neighborhood barriers, economic walls and had created bonds that would last forever.

When the 1961 edition of *Golden Memories* was published near the end of the school year, editors of the school annual offered Ozzie Wadewitz a parting gift of affection by dedicating the yearbook to the beloved coach:

> The successes of our school can be accounted for by the character, determination and enthusiasm of all those who are a member of the school community. For his devotion to Sylvan, his sincere interest in our welfare, his skill as a coach, and his loyalty to the high ideals of the teaching profession and his exemplification of those Christian ideals which have made our school life more meaningful, we dedicate the 1961 Golden Memories to Ozzie Wadewitz.

———

Once stately columns now guard the decaying building that the neighborhood knew as Capitol View Baptist Church.

10

A Flood of Golden Memories

Lee DeFore holds the hands of the old basketball coach with unexpected gentleness. He talks in a soft, melodic voice, reciting familiar names, memorable victories and unforgettable memories. He hands his mentor old newspaper clippings, hoping a headline from the past will make him more aware of the present. He searches Ozzie Wadewitz's vacant face and empty eyes, silently begging for flickers of acknowledgement.

This would be painful for any of the hundreds of young men who played basketball for Wadewitz but it is particularly distressful for DeFore. This is the high school coach that joined a bunch of grade school kids in a sandlot baseball game at Capitol View Elementary School and hit a ball into the trees that DeFore still describes. This is the person that directed a summer day camp at Perkerson Park and made sure DeFore and the other boys got to ride the bus to the downtown YMCA to swim. This is the basketball coach that saw something special in a clumsy ninth grader when no one else did. This is a man who believed in DeFore when the teenager's own faith was threatened. This is the man that changed the course of Lee DeFore's life and the lives of other that he mentored.

Now the two of them are sitting in the lobby of an assisted living center in Sandy Springs. We had planned another visit a few weeks before but the night before we were to go, Ozzie was rushed to the hospital. That episode took a lot out of him, as DeFore soon learns.

Time and declining health has not diminished the bond between Lee DeFore and Ozzie Wadewitz.

When DeFore arrives at the facility in June of 2011, a woman at the receptionist's desk tells him she will call Ozzie and Rosemary's room. Rosemary suffered a stroke in the fall of 2010 and recovery has been slow. Before long, a caretaker pushes Ozzie's metal wheelchair out of the elevator. Ozzie is not really sure who this tall man with the pleasant manner is, but he senses he should know him.

"How did you know I was here?" he asks.

"Angie told me," DeFore tells him.

DeFore is not positive that Ozzie recognizes his daughter's name. A conversation that is cordial but decidedly one-sided slowly begins. Adding to the pain is the feeling that Ozzie has so much to say but can't. He wants to talk about the players, the teams and the ball games that are mentioned but the words will not cooperate. His face is grim. He is frustrated. Logic tells DeFore to go. Love makes him stay.

"Shake my hand, Coach," he says, extending a large right hand.

Ozzie stares. His hand does not move.

"Shake my hand, Coach.

"Shake my hand."

This time DeFore grabs his old coach's right hand. When he does, there are unseen sparks. Ozzie forcefully returns the grip and a smile interrupts the sadness on his face. Again and again, he pumps DeFore's hand.

"My players. My players. My players." Sentences are not complete but his message is delivered. "They would win, win, win."

Questions are asked and he tries so hard to answer. He remembers the players. "Greatest. Greatest. Greatest," he says. "They worked so hard."

"And you were a great coach," DeFore injects.

"Who says?" Ozzie fires back, as a gleam that had not been there before bolts into his eyes.

There is never a true conversation but there is communication. Trying to share stresses the old coach and he starts to sob. Yet, when a caretaker comes to get him, Ozzie waves her away.

I feel like an intruder. I arrived with a camera, two digital recorders, a notebook and a list of questions that were never used. I was going to record words and memories. Instead, I watch a special moment unfold. I stand by Ozzie's wheelchair, as the former player tells him goodbye.

"I never get tired of hearing about my boys," Ozzie says, as the caretaker removes the brake from his wheelchair and pushes him back into the elevator.

THE CLOCK IN life ticks just like the one in a ball game. When they meet, Lee DeFore is 67, with a grandson that is a promising high school basketball player in Alabama. His son, Matt, played on a national championship team at Birmingham-Southern and is about the same age Ozzie was when he passed through DeFore's life more than half a century ago.

Ozzie Wadewitz is 88 years old, stuck in a wheelchair that was never in his game plan. Players from his championship teams now draw Social

Security checks. One of them died much too soon. Neither of the high schools that Ozzie coached in Atlanta exists today. Neither does the school his team defeated for its second state title. Cherished trophies his teams hugged so tightly are gone and so is the wooden case outside the gym that used to house them.

DeFore and Wadewitz are testimonies of how much has changed since Sylvan High School opened in 1950 and how much has transpired since the Golden Bears won those two state championships. It closed as a high school in 1987, adding Sylvan to a long list of closures in the Atlanta Public School System. Over the course of 19 years, 14 of the city's older schools shut their doors: O'Keefe and Dykes (1973); Southwest (1981); George (1984); Roosevelt and Smith (1985); Bass (1987); East Atlanta (1988); Fulton (1990); North Fulton and Northside (1991) and West Fulton and Brown (1992). Some were turned into middle schools. Some were demolished.

Wadewitz observed those things from an unexpected location. He coached in Wisconsin only one season (and Rosemary survived one cruel winter) before realizing he had erred. By then, Bobby Ward had left Capitol View Baptist for a job at 2nd Ponce de Leon Baptist Church. The coach called his longtime friend and said he wanted to get back to Georgia. Northside High Athletic Director Weyman Creel was a member of 2nd Ponce de Leon and Ward told him what the former Sylvan coach said. That led to Wadewitz becoming head coach at Northside — one of Sylvan's fiercest rivals.

His unexpected departure in 1961 altered the basketball universe at Sylvan. Players that dreamed of playing for Wadewitz found former Hogansville High coach Charlie White on the bench instead. Seasons of turmoil lay ahead. "My senior year, our only claim to fame was when we beat Northside on Ozzie's return to a packed Sylvan gym," Baker says.

"White didn't even go into the locker room with us at halftime that night," Copeland says. "He was pouting."

At a reunion of the championship team in 2010, Wadewitz shared a quiet confession with Copeland. "In life, we all make mistakes, and leaving Sylvan was one I made," he said. "We could have won some more games if I had stayed."

An emotional Bob Tuggle speaks at a reunion of the championship teams in 2010. Terry Stephens, Charles Robinson and Tommy Roberts listen to their teammate.

But he didn't.

Stars never really aligned again for the coach, for Sylvan or for Northside. Wadewitz guided the Tigers to three state AA tournaments but the magic was missing. His 1971 team went 24-3 but lost in the state quarterfinals. In 1972, they fell in the opening round. His deepest run came in 1977 when Northside lost to Carver-Atlanta 73-68 in the state AA championship game.

In the decade after Wadewitz's resignation, Sylvan basketball floundered. Problems finally ended with the hiring of Morris Clarke in 1973. He was head coach for 15 years, registering a 188-106 record. He won region titles in 1983, 1984 and 1986 and finished second in 1979 and 1982. His last three teams advanced to the State AA tournament. He also revitalized the baseball program, winning the region in 1973, 1975 and 1976. The baseball Bears were third in the state in 1975 and 1976.

Among his most talented basketball players were Raymond Brown, Maurice (Ezzard) Britain and Jeffrey McFadden. Brown enjoyed a good college career at Mississippi State and the University of Idaho. He is the only Golden Bear to make it to the NBA though his career with the Utah Jazz consisted of one season and 16 games. Britain played on a national junior college championship team at Hutcheson, Kansas and also played a season at Georgia Tech. McFadden starred on Clarke's final Sylvan team averaging 25 points and 15 rebounds a game. He received a scholarship to Auburn University.

Clarke left in 1986 to become assistant principal at Gordon High in DeKalb County. He made the move at a time the status of the school was uncertain. Oliver Banks was his successor. In the final year that Sylvan was a high school, Banks almost accomplished the impossible.

His team lost in the city finals but earned a spot in the 1987 AA state tournament. The Bears, playing with emotion as well as skill, dispatched Decatur, the state's second ranked team, and then upended ninth ranked Central-Carrollton in the semi-finals. That was the final victory in school history.

Sylvan was on a mission but that mission came to an end in the championship game as Lakeshore defeated the Bears 66-58. When the final polls were released, Sylvan, 16-10, was second in the state. Within two months the school was turned into a junior high school.

Coach Steve Daniels coached girl's basketball at Sylvan for 16 years. His teams were powerhouses in the closing years of the high school but never won a state title. The Lady Bears won five consecutive Region 6AA titles and made it to the state playoffs in 1985. These near misses magnify the accomplishments of Ozzie and his band of Bears.

WHITE-FLIGHT DRAMATICALLY changed the makeup of neighborhoods around the high school. A black female that graduated from Sylvan in 1973 came back to a football game that next fall and recalls that the school's black-white ratio had flipped. "It was like everybody moved out of the neighborhood over the summer," she says.

It still does not sound right to hear it called a middle school.

It was first desegregated and then predominantly black. But those changes did not alter the pride people felt in Sylvan High. Near the end of the 1986 school year, more than 100 parents and students demonstrated outside the building to protest the conversion to a middle school. By then, enrollment had dropped from 1,200 students to less than 600.

Bertha Leffall, president of the Sylvan PTA, called on the school board to establish special academic programs at the school rather than convert it. She said the school remained outstanding, because of strong discipline and because "we don't have drugs flowing there." Showing how rigid he could be, principal Ted Jones said though the protest was peaceful students that participated would be punished for missing class.

The school remained a school but nearby streets sometimes felt like war zones. While some pockets of homes were prepared for armed combat, others managed to stay vibrant and comfortable, as a 1992 article in the Journal-Constitution reported.

"People here are committed to neighborliness and brotherhood," commented resident Gerri Corbin of the Neighborhood Planning Unit. "It is a wonderful area for people who are practical about those things that have to do with homeownership and community and how to get the most for your money."

Longtime resident Leslie Long recalled the 1960s and beyond, observing that Sylvan Hills was once THE place to live. Along the way, it became a well-kept secret. "When people come out and look at this neighborhood, they all say: 'I just didn't know that this was here,'" Long noted. However, even staunch supporters did not pretend the area was in the same pristine condition it was in the past.

Harkening back to the sales pitches used by developers in 1923, residents promoted the area as an affordable option for buyers that could not afford such tony neighborhoods as Virginia-Highlands or Morningside.

As established residents grew older, upscale yuppies purchased their properties and revitalized original bungalows in Adair, Capitol View Manor and Sylvan Hills. They did the same with the ranch-style houses on either side of Brewer Boulevard. These homes were saved and they survive even now. But when former residents drive the streets of their childhoods they wonder when the houses got so small and when they got so old.

The problem spots and danger zones are along Stewart Avenue — as old-timers still call it — and on Dill Avenue. A change of name to Metropolitan Parkway around the time of the Atlanta Olympics in 1996 has done nothing to improve Stewart Avenue's image or its reputation.

Nor has there been appreciable change on Dill Avenue or the streets that connect it with Deckner Avenue since an article by Journal-Constitution reporter Milo Ippolito in 2002. His lead paragraphs graphically describe the deplorable scene on Dill Avenue.

> On Dill Avenue, neighbors stop and say hello, merchants chat with prostitutes and homeowners have a quiet understanding with people they suspect are drug dealers.
>
> This Main Street of sorts runs through a gentrifying southwest Atlanta neighborhood where undercover policemen recently shot two prostitutes the officers said had attacked them. The area has been widely known as a place to buy drugs and sex. More recently, it has become a place to buy an affordable house.
>
> "As far as being dangerous, I feel safer on Dill Avenue than I do in Buckhead," said Rebecca Capps, president of

the Capitol View Neighborhood Association, which includes Dill Avenue. "Yes, I do see dealers, and I do see prostitutes every day, and I'm not afraid of them."

Not all residents are so tolerant.

"It bothers me when I come out in the morning time and I see condoms on the street and I have to seep them up," said Joyce Sheperd, chairwoman of Neighborhood Planning Unit X ...

Optimistic suburbanites and buyers who invested in homes or businesses make it sound like Sesame Street. For them, Dill Avenue is a place where people meet on the sidewalk or share garden vegetables with the folks next door.

"If newcomers become part of the neighborhood, criminals leave them alone," said James Byrd, a real estate agent who divides his time between a home office on Dill Avenue and a residence in Midtown. "You speak to them. You treat them with respect. They speak to you. They treat you with respect."

The Dollar Menu King does business in the former location of Parramore's Pharmacy.

Attention was focused on that area at that particular time because of the demolition of Chocolate City, a sleazy nightclub with a parking lot where sex and drugs were for sale 24 hours a day. On a roadway known for raunch, the club had become a nuisance and a pest. City and state officials were on hand for a photo op when bulldozers pushed the walls of the club to the ground in the summer of 2002. "Real estate values don't go up when you have a Chocolate City in your neighborhood," State Rep. Douglas Dean noted as the building began to crumble.

My generation is also familiar with that address. The property where the nightclub was located was the original site of Funtown, an amusement park next to the 24-hour bowling center that opened in the late 1950s. Funtown was a popular spot for young people from Sylvan and other nearby high schools and a place where we enjoyed recording artists such as Tommy Roe and The Isley Brothers.

Funtown would be all but forgotten today were its memory not preserved in Martin Luther King Jr.'s *Letter from the Birmingham Jail*. Written in 1963, this historic piece of literature explains the emotions of the Civil Rights Movement to, of all people, African American clergymen. The loquacious King talked of finding his tongue twisting and his speech stammering as he had to explain to his 6-year-old daughter why she could not go to Funtown. He described "depressing clouds of inferiority begin to form in her little mental sky, and see her distort her little personality by unconsciously developing a bitterness toward white people."

Nearly 40 years after King wrote those words the elected officials that celebrated the demise of that seamy nightclub were black and so were the managers of Chocolate City. Most of the prostitutes that haunted the nearby area were black and so were the people they preyed upon. Many of the property owners were white, however.

State Sen. Vincent Fort lived around Sylvan Hills in 2002. He hoped eradication of that club would lead to better days. "It's kind of darkness at the dawning," he said. "I think some real good things are going to happen."

A decade later, residents still wait for those good things to happen. Dill Avenue remains on the edge of crime and filth and as you drive Metropolitan Parkway, you have an uncommon urge to wash your hands.

The same day we visit Coach Wadewitz, DeFore and I ride the streets of our former neighborhoods. We check out hangouts and haunts and DeFore points to houses in Capitol View Manor and calls the names of classmates that used to live there. We do not know who lives there now and we can only hope their lives are as peaceful as ours were.

Words are my living but it is difficult to put into words the sadness that overcomes us as we sit in a parking lot across from Capitol View Baptist Church. Beautiful stain glass windows in the sanctuary are covered by faceless plywood. Paint is pealing off the stately columns that guard the original entrance. That metal fire escape on the back of the church where DeFore and Ronnie Dodson got in trouble dangles helplessly in the air. The church gym that was important to so many of us is gone. Only a slab remains.

We heard that the beautiful old church might be rescued but that deal is crumbling, just like the church on the corner. A contract was signed with the L.E.A.D. Network, an organization that promotes baseball as an attractive sport for young African American males. This is the group that that nurtured Jason Heyward of the Atlanta Braves. Sandy Thames Kicklighter and Sheri Thames Killam, along with their former next-door neighbor Jerry Baker grew up across the old gym. They helped bring the interested parties together. That deal has cooled and we can only pray for the future of this proud old church.

DeFore and I take Dill Avenue, toward the high school and it is depressing. Dilapidated stores around Sylvan and Dill are monuments to the past and relics of the future. The only familiar sign advertises the chiropractic services of Dr. Eugene Sparlin — a fixture at that corner since 1954. We stop at the traffic light. It is mid-afternoon. If this were midnight, we would lock the doors to our cars.

ROBBIE COTNEY IS an optimist. He moved from Columbus to operate a hardware store in East Atlanta and has lived on Athens Avenue for seven years. He has seen prostitutes hike up their skirts to advertise their merchandise, dodged pit bulls running loose on the streets and has watched dead bodies being loaded into the back of the coroner's van. He has also made wonderful friends and Cotney boasts that Athens Avenue is one of the better streets in Capitol View. Though it is nicer than it was, he admits that it still has a long way to go — a description that fits neighborhoods around the old high school.

"Each one has an active neighborhood association and each is considered to be some of Atlanta's most diverse communities, although not always unified," Cotney says. "The push to rid the area of deeply embedded crime and concerns over rampant gentrification have caused serious tensions within the community. Our area took quite a gut punch when the real estate bubble burst. The 30310 Zip Code already lead the nation in mortgage fraud and the downtown in the real estate industry resulted in foreclosures, auctions and even more vacant houses. One step forward and two steps back."

In Cotney's eyes, the area's major asset — as it has always been — is Perkerson Park. With more than 55 acres, the park is one of the largest green spaces in the city of Atlanta and a place that everyone who lives nearby enjoys. "We held a festival and fundraiser for the park in 2010 and it was a total success, not only as a charity but as a unifying force. It was a fantastic tool for bringing surrounding neighborhoods together with the common goal of enhancing our fantastic park."

Residents like Cotney work hard but so do the criminal elements that want to restore the influence they once had on the neighborhoods around the park. The struggle to keep this area safe and livable is constant. Though it may never be what it was when Sylvan High School was flourishing, it is home to the people who live there.

Retired contractor Earl Shell does not share Cotney's optimism. By the time he was 12, growing up on Kathewood Drive, Shell carried two *Atlanta Journal* routes in Sylvan Hills. As a teen-ager, he added an *Atlanta Constitution* route in the morning. When he was he playing basketball and baseball in high school, he hired younger boys to deliver his newspapers. He knew the neighborhood and the neighborhood knew him.

As a seventh grader at Sylvan Elementary, he was on the School Safety Patrol and his assignment was to help children cross Sylvan Road at Melrose Drive, including 5-year-old Gary Claborn, who as a Sylvan senior in 1962 was president of the student body. These chores gave Shell a perspective of the neighborhood and the people who lived there that most boys his age did not have.

After graduating from Georgia Tech and becoming a successful Atlanta businessman, Shell moved away from the south side and went back less and less. Through real estate ventures and their common passion for Tech, he became close friends with former Yellow Jacket quarterback Kim King, who grew up in West End. In his fifties, the vibrant developer and broadcaster was diagnosed with first cancer and then leukemia.

For years, Shell, Kim King and the former Brown High star's brother Buddy had a standing weekly lunch date. As Kim's health worsened, those lunches became sporadic. Shell sensed the end was near for his friend but he was pleasantly surprised one day in 2004 when Buddy called and said Kim wanted him to pick them up for lunch.

A week before King's death, they went to a favorite spot in College Park. During the meal, Kim asked Shell about growing up in Sylvan Hills. Leaving the restaurant, Kim asked his friend to take him by the neighborhood where he grew up.

"I didn't think he was serious, but I finally crossed the tracks near Fort McPherson. I drove down Langston to Kathewood and I was immediately struck by the total lack of trees. Many of the houses had plywood on the windows. I drove slowly, looking for our old house. I went three houses past it and had to back up. I didn't recognize my own house. That night, I told my wife I would never go back to Sylvan Hills again."

Our generations hold on to the way we saw those neighborhoods when we were young. It is difficult for us to accept these special places the way they are now. However blighted the area is when we visit today, we have to keep in mind that at a crucial time in our lives this humble part of town was our anchor and our refuge. It is our history, and even if we can't accept it, we must embrace it.

These various golden memories connect us to a time that lives on in musty yearbooks and fading copies of the school paper. They have been reinvigorated by quarterly gatherings at The Varsity and by exchanges on social networking sites such as Facebook.com and Classmates.com. Events at the Varsity have grown so large that they have split into two groups.

"We talk about our neighborhood roots," says Herb Britt, a student on Sylvan High's first day of school more than 60 years ago. "The high school was a big part of that. These were good neighborhoods to grow up in. Transportation was poor and there was not a lot of money but we hung in there together."

Britt laughs about a common practice on the football team that was not unusual for that era. Coaches did not believe their players should drink water at practices or in games. Dehydration was not in the football vocabulary.

"We'd all suck on the towel — and it was the same wet towel," he says. "Everybody, and I mean everybody sucked on it."

Residents of Sylvan Hills, Capitol View and Adair Park also sucked on the same towel. None of us were particularly rich and none of us would admit to being poor. No one's house was that much than larger than their neighbor's and nobody's automobile was flashier than the car parked outside the house next door. Our fathers went to church on Sunday morning and to work on Mondays. Commonalities such as these led to strong bonds in the neighborhoods, the churches and at the high school.

Norma McLendon says the Sylvan faculty enjoyed similar bonds, though we never thought about such things when we were younger. We knew them only as teachers. They were ageless and what they did after school was a mystery. We never stopped to think that they had lives of their own.

When we visited in 2011, the retired teacher was rehabbing from a stroke at Christian City, south of the Atlanta airport. You could call us peers and friends but to me she will always be Mrs. McLendon. She came to the high school to teach English in 1955 and stayed more than 25 years. She was part of a faculty that grew old together. They taught together, reared families together and shared problems together. She says the glue that bound them together was the neighborhood and the people that lived there.

"It was a wonderful time and a wonderful place," she says. "No one was rich and no one was poor. Families went to church on Sundays so values were strong. We were blessed with talented students that went to Harvard and Yale and West Point. We were there at a wonderful time in history."

For years, she was faculty advisor for *The Bear Facts*, the student newspaper. As a teacher of English she believed in writing. That carried over to the newspaper. I was asked to write a piece about the meaning of Christmas in my junior year and the following year I became feature editor of the paper. Never did I imagine that this would be my career and my life.

"I should say thank you to teachers like you every day," I told her as I was leaving.

"No," she answered. "It is us who should be thanking you."

AS YOUNG PEOPLE, we were shielded from society's changing mores. But in the 1960s, our Ozzie and Harriet world started to topple. Mothers had to go to work. Fathers took a second job. Parking became an issue around the high school because so many of us suddenly had cars. War in a place called Vietnam made letters from Ameilia Estes at the local draft board something to fear. Georgia Gov. Ernest Vandiver threatened to close the public schools because of integration and we wondered — if Sylvan High did not close — what would it be like to have a black student sit next to us in second period English?

The stability and bonds prevalent at home and the uninterrupted continuity found at the high school helped the neighborhood cope with the changes society was forcing on us. The outside world was constantly evolving but in many ways the school was not. John Agnew, who graduated from Sylvan in 1969, explains the importance of that continuity.

"Many neighborhoods such as Adair Park (where the Agnews grew up) still had third and even fourth generations living there. Our grandparents had raised their families on those same streets. Stewart Avenue United Methodist Church just celebrated its centennial in 2009, and families of the founders still stay in close contact. Even the faculty at Sylvan had many teachers and administrators that had been there for years. Being the youngest of four, by the time I reached the eighth grade I felt like I already knew many of those people. I had heard all the stories and nicknames and I thought of them as 'celebrities.'"

Sylvan's cafeteria has been modernized but that doesn't keep students from complaining about the food.

Agnew also describes the friendships that developed between parents and the high school faculty. These ties enforced discipline at school because we realized that our teachers knew how to reach our Mom and Dad if we got out of line. Through the years, Agnew's father became friends with Rufus Burger, the school's longtime Latin teacher. That relationship developed during those annual PTA meetings where parents followed their child's class schedule.

"Mr. Burger was my homeroom teacher and after many years of that event, he and my Dad became buddies. My folks would start in homeroom. Then, while my Mom followed my class schedule, my Dad would hang out in Mr. Burger's room. That may have been the only way my mother could convince my father to go."

The fear of integration at Sylvan was raised when we got to school one morning in 1960 or 1961. A mysterious white-supremacy flyer had been slipped into every student locker at Sylvan. No one knew who put the inflammatory documents in there but with leaders of the Ku Klux Klan living nearby there must have been many suspects.

To escape the fear of the unknown, students — particularly girls — started taking classes in summer school so they could graduate early. Some parents enrolled their sons at Georgia Military Academy in College Park, not knowing how they were going to afford the steep tuition. Graduating classes in 1960, 1961 and 1962 were turned upside down by these shuffles.

The United States Supreme Court outlawed school segregation in 1954 when it ruled on Brown v. Board of Education. It took seven years of litigation, bickering and outrageous commentary for it to become a reality in the Atlanta public schools. After years of rhetoric, it came quietly on August 30, 1961 when nine African American students enrolled at Brown, Murphy, Grady and Northside. It was just another first day of school. The peacefulness was reported nationally and was mentioned by President John F. Kennedy during a White House press conference.

Desegregation did not come to Sylvan until the latter stages of the 1960s. It too was peaceful. No crosses were burned. There were no marches. But there were natural changes. Black faculty members were added to the staff and the racial makeup of the student body soon became an issue. As it was in the neighborhood, the ratio of black to white in the student body did not change overnight. But within a decade the historically white school was predominantly black and the tranquility of the past was threatened.

Pride was still there, however. Young people continued to get an education. Cheerleaders danced around at pep rallies and bonfires and the band still played Robert Jenkins' old fight song. White flight and an aging populace led to drastic drops in enrollment and rumors of the school's demise circulated throughout the decade.

During the 1986-1987 school year, the school board pulled the plug on Sylvan just as it did other historic high schools in the city. It closed as a high school in June and reopened as a middle school in September. When the end came, African American students and parents mourned the loss of the high school alongside older white alumni.

On Facebook.com, there are several Sylvan pages. One covers the middle school years. One is for people that graduated when the school was young and the paint was fresh. People that graduated there during the final years of the high school frequent another one of the sites. It saddens me to read comment after comment from students of that latter era lamenting that so many of their classmates keep meeting violent deaths.

Those of us that graduated in the past also mourn friends from our days at Sylvan. Our classmates fight cancer or suffer heart attacks or just die of old age. We say a prayer and look into the face of our own mortality. Marking death must be dramatically different for those younger grads. How tragic it must be to hear that a young person you knew in school has been murdered.

And the only things we have in common are diplomas from Sylvan High School.

TIME HAS NOT been kind to the building that was Sylvan High. On the surface, little has changed. It looks pretty good for its age. On the inside, the skeleton is crumbling. Moisture has crept into the walls. Mysterious odors regularly invade the lower floor without warning. It is hard to heat and expensive to cool. Maintenance must be practiced one day at a time. How long the aging structure can survive, no one knows.

Parts of the building have received facelifts. Parts are just as we left it. The cafeteria is modernized but it is a safe guess that students still whine about the quality of the food. The media center — the room we called a library — has been completely redone. A new wing of classrooms and offices has been added since I was a student but musty restrooms are a journey into the past that you take at your own risk. The principal's office has hardly changed, though the names on the door have. If those walls could speak, the stories they could tell. Walk into the clinic and you expect Nurse Savage to ask what ails you.

Lee DeFore had not been there in 40-something years so when the middle school principal tells us we are welcome to roam the halls we do. School is out for the summer so we're almost alone. As we walk, we remember teachers that haunted the empty classrooms.

Naturally, we end up in the lobby of the gym. We walk up the steps, past the concession stand where popcorn and soft drinks were sold and through the foreboding doors on to the floor of the gym.

"It still smells the same," DeFore comments.

Only a ball player would notice that and only a former player would tiptoe around the glistening hardwood floor searching for his favorite spots to shoot. DeFore walked into the gymnasium a 67-year-old grandfather. On that court, at that moment, he is a 17-year-old kid with an automatic jump shot.

While we talk about games that were played in that building, a group of men in work clothes joins us at the other end of the floor. As they walk toward us, one of them takes notice of DeFore.

"I'll bet you scored some baskets in here," he says — a safe observation when you are talking to a man who is nearly 6-foor-7. The other men leave but Charlie Walker stays behind. Walker is Sylvan's chief of maintenance, a demanding job when you are in charge of a building that old. He is from Tennessee and a Vietnam veteran. Sylvan has been his assignment for nearly 15 years.

"You know the folks downtown want to tear it down, don't you? Walker says, not hiding his own feelings about that. "We'll be here next year, but that will probably be it."

Demolition is not his idea. He has been there long enough to call every brick by name. Walker's affection for that building and that school is deep and genuine. At the same time, he knows Sylvan is running out of time and the Atlanta school system is running out of money. Enrollment continues to drop and the cost of upkeep continues to rise. Such a combination can mean only one thing.

"They'd level it tomorrow if they could," Walker says.

As we leave the gym, we ask about the trophy case that used to be across from the concession stand. It is gone and so are trophies, plaques and awards that once upon a time were displayed in that case.

"I've been here 15 years, and I don't remember any trophies," he says. A former Sylvan principal told me the state championship trophies and the Golden Bear statue were stored in the basement. Walker shakes his head no. That is not good news, for if anyone would know the whereabouts of those missing trophies, it would be Charlie Walker.

As we talk, he walks us through the building, unlocking closed classrooms and asking us what we think of the school now. When we tell him how good it looks, he says thank you. In him, there is a pride of ownership that you do not find in many employees today. His tour takes us to the library.

"I didn't spend much time in here," DeFore jokes.

We ask whether old school yearbooks might be stowed away somewhere. Walker does not know the answer but DeFore does. He finds an unlocked closet at the rear of the room where past copies of *Golden Memories* are randomly stacked. We take a few editions to a table and Walker is as interested as we are. He wants to see his building when it was young.

FIFTY YEARS AGO, when that aging schoolhouse was less than 10 years old, its rafters were shaken several times a week by the roar of crowds that shoved their way into the gym. Games were won and so were titles. For members of those championship teams, those were life-changing moments.

Those young men — though they did not understand it then — provided moments to remember for their proud families, for people in the stands, for teachers that did not come to that many games and for folks that every morning and afternoon religiously followed Sylvan games through the pages of the sports section.

Even lowly sub-freshmen just beginning the high school journey got caught up in the action. "I started to Sylvan in 1960," Carla Putnam Veal says. "I got caught up in the spirit right away. I'll never forget the experience of going to that championship game. When you're in the eighth grade, you think such things happen every year."

John Agnew did not come along until later. He is a 1969 Sylvan graduate but he still feels a connection to those basketball seasons, as do many others that were too young to get to very many games. On the night Sylvan defeated LaGrange for that first title in 1960, Agnew was 8 years old, holding tight to a small transistor radio.

By the time the Bears won those titles, 1956 Sylvan basketball star Earl Shell was a senior at Georgia Tech. He went to the tournament games and was standing with Ozzie Wadewitz when Grady coach W.O. Skelton congratulated him for a victory that put Sylvan in the championship game for the second year in a row. "The coach asked Ozzie how it felt to coach a team and know that not only are you going to win every night but win big?"

Many people saw that team as invincible. Walter F. George coach Pat Stephens said they weren't human. This kind of hyperbole still surprises former players that every day saw humanity in their teammates. Ronnie Dodson got a glimpse of how the team is viewed in 2010 at a Seniors Golf Tournament in Thomaston. "We were at a cookout and this fellow asked me if I went to Sylvan High. I thought he must have gone to school with me but he said, no, he went to Southwest High. He played on the basketball team there and said that all he remembers is that we beat the snot out of them that year."

For the players, trying to explain or express what those championship seasons mean to them is much more difficult than trying to beat that Ashland Tom Cat press was so very long ago.

Terry Stephens told teammates they became his family. Seated are Billy Seabrook, Ronnie Dodson and Bob Tuggle.

When Terry Stephens tries to do that his mind goes back to the dressing room at Alexander Memorial Coliseum. "On that last night, after we won the second championship, Coach Wadewitz told us we had done something people would never forget. He said it would take us about 10 years before we fully understood what we had done. He was right too."

Tommy Roberts cannot help but remember how much fun they had together. "It is something to be proud of. As you get older, you realize how few people ever get a chance to play for one state championship — and we played for two. It is something we won't forget."

Lee DeFore is honest about those championships. "I'm not sure we were the best team in the state that first year — just the best team that week. But in 1961, we were definitely the best."

Bob Tuggle says the experiences reset the course of his life. "We had no concept then how important that event was to our lives. If I hadn't been part of that team, I probably wouldn't have gone to college. Without that history, no one would have wanted me."

Ronnie Dodson is thankful for what he learned about living. "Ozzzie taught us a lot about life. You don't realize how much you learned until you're over the age of 50. He taught us the importance of teamwork, in basketball and in the world. That is what we carry with us today."

The framework of a team was important to them 50 years ago. At that age, you assume it will always be that way. But when the Class of 1961 put on caps and gowns and left Sylvan High behind, the seniors on the squad chose individual paths. Younger teammates followed over the next two years. The fact that so many of them went on to play and participate at the next level shows how talented and committed Ozzie's boys were:

- Lee DeFore received a scholarship to Auburn University. His resume is long. He lettered three years and was team captain his senior year. His 23.7 scoring average led the SEC in 1967. He left as the school's all-time leading scorer and he still ranks 12th with 1,386 points. The New York Knicks drafted him in the fourth round.

- Tommy Roberts turned down a football scholarship to Clemson University and accepted a basketball scholarship to Georgia Tech. After a red-shirt year, he was a starter for the Yellow Jackets in 1964. When Tech and Auburn met that season, he and DeFore faced each other for the first time. Academic issues ended Roberts' career prematurely.

- Terry Stephens played at LaGrange College. He was All-GIAC in 1962. After two years as a starter there, he transferred to Georgia State.

- Bob Tuggle also played at LaGrange College. Like Stephens, he transferred to Georgia State where he and Virlyn Gaynes were co-captains of the 1964 Panther team.

- Virlyn Gaynes went to Middle Georgia Junior College and then to Georgia State where he showed he could score as well as rebound. He led the Panthers in scoring and rebounding two straight years.

- Ronnie Dodson and Charles (Checkers) Robinson played two years at Middle Georgia Junior College.

- Bart Hickman played as a walk-on at Georgia State University.

- Billy Seabrook received a football scholarship to Vanderbilt University.

- Steve Copeland signed a football scholarship to Georgia Tech but transferred to Jacksonville State University where he was a four-year starter in basketball.

- Jerry Baker was a walk-on at the University of Georgia.
- Wilson Culbreath played baseball at West Georgia College.
- Charles Jordan, a reserve on the 1960 champions, was a scholarship football player at Georgia Tech.
- Bill England, so valuable as the student manager, assumed a similar role as a student at LaGrange College. After a career in journalism, he went into sports administration at Valdosta State College.

Virlyn Gaynes 1943-1989

As their college years ended, teammates that had been so close drifted apart. Business careers took them far from Sylvan Hills and Atlanta and far from fellows so important to their past. Many of them came together in 1989 for the unexpected funeral of an important teammate. Virlyn Gaynes was standing at the rear of his car pumping gas at a convenience store when he was felled by a heart attack.

A freakish ability to jump is how most people remember Gaynes — a memory that his son David understands in his own way. "I inherited that jumping ability and I'm watching my boys to see if they have those genes," he says David Gaynes had an outstanding college career at Emory University and is a member of school's Athletic Hall of Fame" — along with legends such as golfer Bobby Jones.

Teammates remember Virlyn's tenacious spirit and the way he could make them laugh. Maybe it was his premature death or maybe the time had come, but whatever the reason old teammates started to rekindle old friendships. They could no longer run up and down a basketball court but they could play golf, so once or twice a year a golf weekend was planned.

Their group slowly expanded to include Sylvan people that were not on the basketball team and even though I gave up golf long ago I joined them for a weekend on a Robert Trent Jones Golf Courses near Auburn University in the spring of 2006. It was the first time I had seen those guys in years and the first time I heard stories of those championship seasons shared by the players that wrote them.

When Bill England walked into dinner in a Sylvan letter sweater that used to be white, I was shocked. But unlike some of us in that room, he could still fit into his old sweater. Around the table were men whose hair was gray. Flattop haircuts and flat bellies were part of history. One of them wore a hearing aid and several others should have. More than one was a cancer survivor and a few of them were married to girls that used to stand and cheer on the sidelines at Sylvan basketball games.

After dinner, scrapbooks that their mothers kept for them when they were young were produced. Every item inspired a story that had to be told. One fellow would start the story and somebody else would finish it. When someone mentioned a victory over Baker High School, Steve Copeland looked over at me.

"Tell 'em about Bubba," he said.

Bubba Ball was the coach of the Lions in 1960. He was already a legend, having coached the Columbus school to two state basketball titles. By 2006, old Bubba was somewhere in his eighties. I told them that he had a couple of sons in high school.

"Way to go, Bubba," DeFore exclaimed.

When the subject of the game with Ashland, Ky., came up, I told them about conversations I had about that game. The day after Ashland gave Sylvan its only defeat in 1961, a bunch of us civilians were playing ball on the outside court next to the school. Ashland had a practice session at the Sylvan gym and afterward some players wandered over to where we were.

I complimented their speed and defense.

"Yeah, and we left our two black starters at home," one of the guys from Kentucky said.

Many years later, former University of Kentucky basketball player Larry Conley moved into my apartment complex in Atlanta. He played on that Ashland team and I told him about that conversation. "Those guys were pulling your leg," the popular television commentator said. "We didn't have any black starters."

There we were in a hotel hospitality room across the street from Auburn University, talking about a high school basketball game in Atlanta that most people had forgotten. Guys in that room remembered it though. That loss hurts them more today than it did back then. Being able to talk about a perfect season would be so much better than replaying one that is 36-1.

Numbers from that 1961 season are important to them.

- Sylvan won 40 games in a row over Georgia teams.
- Sylvan averaged 77.4 points a game.
- Sylvan held opponents to 45.9 points a game.
- Sylvan's margin of victory was 28.5 points a game.
- Sylvan scored more than 100 points twice.
- Sylvan scored more than 90 points five times.

The 74.4 points a game Sylvan averaged in 1961 was achieved when games were 32 minutes long, when there was no 3-point basket and when teams did not have to beat a shot clock. That 74.4 average would have been even higher if Sylvan's 29-17 win over North Fulton was discounted. A power failure ended that game prematurely in the second quarter. Eliminate it from the stats, and Sylvan's per game average would be an amazing 77.9.

Tommy Roberts (left) was MVP of the state AAA Tournament in 1960 and teammate Lee DeFore won the following year.

More than once, Tommy Roberts has asked me whether Sylvan's 36 wins in 1961 could be a state record. The answer is that nobody really knows. High school football statistics in Georgia are reasonably complete. Basketball records are not so accurate.

"There is football and then there is everything else. Extensive basketball records just do not exist," explains Steve Figueroa, director of media relations for the Georgia High School Association. The GHSA is the governing body for high school sports, in charge of events from public speaking to football so Figueroa has access to the official records. He also edited a statewide high school sports magazine and was a longtime sports writer for newspapers in Georgia. In a court of law, he would be an expert witness. For him to say such records do not exist is almost the final word.

Like Figueroa I have searched Microfilm of Georgia papers for many years so I understand when he talks about spotty coverage. Reporters pay attention to high school basketball only after the last football game. For that reason, you cannot count on the won-loss records they write about. They are at the mercy of coaches that do not count the games their team plays until after their football players start playing. These weaknesses in reporting make records shaky. "I can tell you who the state champions were going all the way back, but the history books don't tell us what a team's win-loss record was," Figueroa says.

A current GHSA rule precludes contemporary basketball teams from winning 36 games, Figueroa points out. High school teams in Georgia can play no more than 25 games in a season. This includes holiday tournaments, region championships and the state playoffs. This rule has been in effect for around 20 years.

These things, along with a search through the records and old files that are available, lead me to believe that the Golden Bears' victory total should be considered a state record.

Comparing individual basketball teams is more difficult than comparing win-loss records. No one has yet discovered a process that would do that successfully. However, several years ago, a reporter with the Journal-Constitution wrote an article that purportedly ranked the greatest high school basketball teams in Georgia history. That is a dangerous task, one that makes only one school and one group of fans completely happy. The only things they accomplish is an increase in conversation and blood pressure.

The story did not mention Sylvan High School.

Months after the article appeared, at a gathering of Sylvan players in Oxford, Ala., hurt feelings were expressed when someone mentioned that story. They accomplished things no other Georgia team had ever accomplished. They won 36 games and won them decisively. When the subject of high school basketball in this state is discussed, what they did in two championship runs must be remembered.

Actually, no one can accurately rank basketball teams, particularly teams from different eras and especially teams that played before desegregation. The history of high school basketball was totally rewritten with the appearance of the first black players and teams in 1967. I worked at the state tournament that year and after Beach of Savannah's championship run I was not struck by the fact their skin was black but by the distinct change in style and strategy they brought to Alexander Memorial Coliseum. Beach soundly defeated South Fulton, another all-black team from East Point. South Fulton was ponderous. They walked the ball up court wearing matching scowls. Beach wore a smile and they never stopped running. That would be the way basketball would be played for years to come.

How would the Sylvan five compete in such an era? I will not make the same mistakes the Atlanta writer did. I do not think you can conclusively say any single high school team is the best of all time. At the same time, I could not leave the Golden Bears off any short list of great high school teams in Georgia history. They deserve recognition.

Sylvan's relentless style of play on both ends of the court would blend well in today's world. Their lineup included a deadly spot-up shooter in Lee DeFore and a slasher in Tommy Roberts. The individual style of Virlyn Gaynes was ahead of its time. If they had grown up playing that tempo of basketball, Terry Stephens and Bob Tuggle would effectively fit today's game. The speed and quick hands of Ronnie Dodson would be even more valuable today than it was then. Steve Copeland would get more minutes because of a need for additional rebounding. A half-court offense would be pertinent making Charles Robinson's shooting an asset.

Would they finish with a 36-1 record if they were playing today? Probably not. Would they contend for the state championship? Yes they would. Would they be exciting to watch? I think it safe to say they would be more exciting to watch than they were 50 years ago because their opponents would not be playing in slow motion.

These observations are pure conjecture. More important is what these players did accomplish. They won 71 games in three years, and did so with class and grace and confidence that never approached arrogance. Families were proud and so were the people who cheered them. At a time high school basketball in Georgia was threatening to explode Sylvan High lit the fuse. What they achieved is magical. They burst on to the scene as unknowns with little expected of them and left as champions. They came back the following year with expectations on their shoulders and targets on their backs and they won again. They ought to be remembered and they must be respected.

NOTHING IN THE old schoolhouse or the old neighborhoods honors what this basketball team did for a side of town that for so long hungered for recognition and pride. No one knows where the championship trophies are today, or if they even exist. Even the wooden case that housed the awards is gone. No banners hang from the rafters of the aging gym where they played and alumni and friends resign themselves to the fact that their high school is on a collision course with a wrecking ball.

Members of the 1960 and 1961 state championship squad gather around Coach Ozzie Wadewitz for a team picture during the team's first reunion in 2010. Kneeling is Bart Hickman. On the first row are Ronnie Dodson, Terry Stephens, Jerry Baker, Wilson Culbreath, Tommy Roberts and Team Manager Bill England. On the back row are Billy Seabrook, Charles Robinson, Bob Tuggle, Lee DeFore and Steve Copeland.

When demolition finally comes — and it will — we will mourn but we will not be alone in our grief. Around the country, changing neighborhoods have led to changing schools. Abandoned schoolhouses become mausoleums and then they go away. It is part of the urban dance. In Columbus, where I have lived since 1972, I have written about the affection old grads have for the old Baker High School and have noted how similar their feelings are to our attachments to Sylvan.

I spent time at Baker during its final week as a high school. I wrote about hundreds of trophies that were left behind and how the principal intended to trash them. The next day players from the Lions' state championship basketball teams retrieved them as mementoes. So did members of the school's title-winning track teams. A granite lion that guarded the front of the school was also saved. In 2011, when the massive building was taken down, former students rescued stacks of red brick that once were Baker along with a marble plaque and the flagpole that stood in front of the old school.

Such dramas have been played out over and over again around the country as graduates of former high schools fight to hold on to pieces of their past. Some have even taken their fight to rescue old trophies to their local school officials.

We may have waited too long at Sylvan. Trophies and awards are missing and probably destroyed, though 1962 graduate Jean Hankinson Zuniga continues to bulldog a search for the missing pieces of our past. She is relentless. Like her, I hate to think these things that were once so cherished were thrown into a dumpster, but I also wonder what we would do with them if they are found.

More important than the trophies are things that can be preserved. These attributes are found within us. As we look back at where we came from, we acknowledge the nurturing and care this high school and these neighborhoods provided us when we were young and needed them most.

We are older now, so we appreciate this support in ways we never imagined when we were teen-agers. We laugh about the good times and brush away the bad. Whatever year we graduated, we are proud of the Sylvan High School we attended and marvel that with all our mischief and mayhem we learned as much as we did. We appreciate our foundation and build on it every day.

We can't go home, but we will never leave.

———

Appendix

SYLVAN HIGH FOOTBALL THROUGH THE YEARS

At a Glance

Overall Record: 171-187-15 .479

State Titles: 0

Conference Titles: 0

Region Titles: 1 (Region 6-A (1976)

All-State Players: 8

NFL Players: 1

Weeks Ranked No. 1: 18

Longest win streak: 15 (Oct. 24, 1975 to Nov. 19, 1976)

Longest losing streak 13 (Sept. 2, 1978 to Sept. 21, 1979)

Head Coaches

Jimmy Green (1950-1958, 44-40-8)

Jack Wood (1959-1962, 19-21-)

Ed Newby (1963-1964, 14-6-1)

Ray Dean (1965-1970, 17-39-2)

Steve Daniels (1971-1973, 14-15-1)

Willie Hunter (1975-1976, 19-2-1)

Morris Clarke (1977, 3-6-1)

Ronald Brown (1979-1986, 37-42-1)

Season by Season

1950 4-4-2 Jimmy Green

1951 3-7-0 Jimmy Green

1952 4-5-1 Jimmy Green

1953 7-4-0 Jimmy Green

1954 5-5-0 Jimmy Green

1955 5-4-2 Jimmy Green

1956 2-6-2 Jimmy Green

1957 7-3-0 Jimmy Green

1958 7-2-1 Jimmy Green

1959 6-4-0 Jack Wood

1960 5-5-0 Jack Wood

1961 4-6-0 Jack Wood

1962 4-6-0 Jack Wood

1963 4-5-1 Ed Newby

1964 10-1-0 Ed Newby

1965 3-7-0 Ray Dean

1966 4-4-1 Ray Dean
1967 2-7-0 Ray Dean
1968 3-7-0 Ray Dean
1969 2-8-0 Ray Dean
1970 3-6-1 Ray Dean
1971 4-5-1 Steve Daniels
1972 6-4-0 Steve Daniels
1973 4-6-0 Steve Daniels
1974 4-6-0
1975 8-1-1 Willie Hunter
1976 11-1-0 Willie Hunter
1977 3-6-1 Morris Clarke
1978 0-10-0
1979 4-6-0 Ronald Brown
1980 6-4-0 Ronald Brown
1981 5-5-0 Ronald Brown
1982 4-6-0 Ronald Brown
1983 6-4-0 Ronald Brown
1984 3-6-1 Ronald Brown
1985 3-7-0 Ronald Brown
1986 6-4-0 Ronald Brown

Ranked Teams

1953 — 12th Class AA
1957 — 10th Class AAA
1959 — 10th Class AAA
1964 — 10th Class AAA

1975 — 8th Class A
1976 — 7th Class A

Players in All-Star Game

1955 — Rausey Mason T
1959 — Doug Cooper QB and Jim Parks C
1960 — Joe Wolfe E and Bill Paschal T
1963 — Steve Copeland E
1964 — Lee Kidd FB
1965 — Donnie Hampton QB and Beal Lazenby HB
1977 — David Allen RB

All-State Players

Rausey Mason T 1954
Doug Cooper QB 1958
Bill Paschal T 1959
Larry Seabrook T 1963
Beal Lazenby HB 1964
William Judson DB 1976
Kenneth Collins L 1976
David Allen RB 1976

Players in the NFL

William Judson (1976) — Miami Dolphins, (1982-1989)

SYLVAN BASKETBALL
THE CHAMPIONSHIP YEARS

1958-59 (16-10)

Sylvan 58 North Fulton 53
Sylvan 41 College Park 38
Sylvan 51 Marietta 47
Sylvan 72 Fulton 63
Sylvan 49 Sprayberry 33
Sylvan 44 Grady 29
Sylvan 63 Bass 39
Sylvan 52 Campbell-Smyrna 58
Sylvan 55 Smith 54

Tri-City Tournament
Sylvan 63 Fulton 37
Sylvan 54 College Park 43
Sylvan 47 Russell 62

Sylvan 66 West Fulton 62
Sylvan 45 O'Keefe 43
Sylvan 60 Northside 61
Sylvan 53 Southwest 51
Sylvan 41 Roosevelt 55
Sylvan 50 Brown 60
Sylvan 47 West Fulton 30
Sylvan 57 O'Keefe 48
Sylvan 53 Northside 77
Sylvan 36 Southwest 53
Sylvan 50 Roosevelt 52
Sylvan 37 Brown 56

City Tournament
Sylvan 69 Bass 56
Sylvan 53 Murphy 56

1959-60 (20-7)

Sylvan 62 Marietta 61
Sylvan 57 East Atlanta 38
Sylvan 39 Fulton 38
Sylvan 63 Grady 43
Sylvan 46 North Fulton 62
Sylvan 51 Northside 67
Sylvan 52 O'Keefe 46

Tri-City Tournament
Sylvan 65 Headland 41
Sylvan 33 Russell 49

Sylvan 54 Southwest 47
Sylvan 38 West Fulton 33
Sylvan 71 Walter F. George 37
Sylvan 53 Brown 55
Sylvan 49 Northside 60
Sylvan 56 O'Keefe 35
Sylvan 33 Southwest 31
Sylvan 47 West Fulton 56
Sylvan 68 Walter F. George 51
Sylvan 49 Brown 51

City Tournament
Sylvan 47 Roosevelt 45
Sylvan 59 Murphy 40
Sylvan 38 Brown 56
Sylvan 44 North Fulton 36

State AAA Tournament
Sylvan 40 Baker-Columbus 37
Sylvan 41 Campbell-Smyrna 38
Sylvan 57 Brown 45
Sylvan 49 LaGrange 42

1960-61 (36-1)

Sylvan 72 Grady 48

Sylvan 77 Roosevelt 56

Sylvan 29 North Fulton 17

Sylvan 72 Bass 28

Sylvan 65 Murphy 52

Sylvan 65 East Atlanta 30

Sylvan 75 Dykes 36

Sylvan 74 Northside 57

Sylvan 94 Walter F. George 38

Georgia-Kentucky Doubleheaders

Sylvan 64 Newport (KY) 58

Sylvan 68 Ashland (KY) 87

Sylvan 116 Therrell 35

Sylvan 63 Fulton 34

Metropolitan Tournament

Sylvan 72 Walter F. George 28

Sylvan 74 Russell 44

Sylvan 60 Marietta 45

Sylvan 68 Smith 39

Sylvan 87 West Fulton 56

Sylvan 96 Southwest 61

Sylvan 73 O'Keefe 54

Sylvan 79 Brown 47

Sylvan 89 Dykes 51

Sylvan 60 Northside 57

Sylvan 91 Walter F. George 73

Sylvan 101 Therrell 35

Sylvan 79 West Fulton 52

Sylvan 78 Southwest 58

Sylvan 74 O'Keefe 38

Sylvan 79 Brown 51

City 3-AAA Tournament

Sylvan 69 East Atlanta 41

Sylvan 82 Walter F. George 52

Sylvan 87 North Fulton 57

Sylvan 67 Murphy 36

State AAA Tournament

Sylvan 78 Richmond Academy 43

Sylvan 63 Avondale 56

Sylvan 61 Grady 41

Sylvan 62 Campbell-Smyrna 58

Tournament Boxscores 1960

Sylvan (40) Gaynes 6, Roberts 20, DeFore 8, Stephens 4, Tuggle 2

Baker (37) Nixon 2, Waldrop 6 Pritchard 1, Bolden 4, Thomas 12, I. Long 2, Tolbert 8 D. Long, Gunn 2.

Sylvan (41) Gaynes 9, Stephens 2, DeFore 12, Roberts 10, Tuggle 8.

Campbell-Smyrna (38) Pitts 12, Adair 2, Lockridge 7, Beckett 8, Brown 9.

Sylvan (57 Gaynes 10, Roberts 11, DeFore 8, Stephens 13, Tuggle 15.

Brown (45) Ogles 6, Watts 17, Babb 8, Hartsfield 4, Jordan 6, Casey 4, Gibson.

Sylvan (49) Gaynes 11, Roberts 10, DeFore 10, Tuggle 7, Stephens 11.

LaGrange (42) Cheek 14, Fowler 3, Mahaffey 14, Holder 5, Smith 6, Jones.

Tournament Boxscores 1961

Sylvan (78) Tuggle 7, Gaynes 14, DeFore 18, Roberts 12, Stephens 12, Dodson 7, Copeland 6, Baker 2, Seabrook, Robinson, Culbreath.

Richmond Academy (43) Mahon 4, Regan 13, Woodward 7, Murphy 6, Ray 4, Davis 4, Knight 2, Clark 1, Frieberg 2, Wright, Neuhaus, Gray.

Sylvan (63) Tuggle 3, Gaynes, 7, DeFore 30, Roberts 13, Stephens 10.

Avondale (56) Pritchett 8, Martin 19, Guy 19, Cotton 5, Hargrove 5.

Sylvan (64) Tuggle 8, Gaynes 14, DeFore 20, Roberts 18, Stephens 2, Copeland 2, Dodson, Seabrook.

Grady (41) Shuey 4. Fiblekorn 3, Baxter 18, Chaotas 7, Hines 6, Peek 3, Entrekin, Krant, Crawford, Dwiskin, McConnell.

Sylvan (62) Tuggle 9, Gaynes 8, DeFore 15, Roberts 19, Stephens 11.

Campbell-Smyrna (58) Pitts 20, Ramey, Adair 2, Brown 8, Beckett 27, Mann 1, Turner.

Acknowledgements

Looking back, I've been researching this book since I was a junior at Sylvan High School. Watching classmates march to two straight state basketball titles fueled an interest in sports that led me to a lengthy career in journalism.

At reunions of those teams I heard the stories of those magical seasons and I began to realize what an impact those championships had on the players and on the people that cheered their successes. That nugget grew into *Ozzie's Boys* — but before that story could be told others had to contribute memories and support.

This book would not have been published without Lee DeFore. In 1961, he was MVP of the state basketball tournament and he deserves another trophy for what he did for this book. Old photographs of the team contained here came from his family scrapbook. His mother cared enough to purchase pictures from the Journal-Constitution and they are priceless. Lee arranged a meeting with Coach Ozzie Wadewitz that sadly turned into a portrait of the unwavering link between player and coach and, showing love and creativity, he designed the book cover.

Many of his teammates spent hours on the phone with me telling stories — most of them true. That roster includes Tommy Roberts, Terry Stephens, Bob Tuggle, Ronnie Dodson, Billy Seabrook, Steve Copeland, Jerry Baker, Bart Hickman, Charles Robinson and Wilson Culbreath. Team Manager Bill England — like me a refugee from the newspaper business — added his own reflections.

My friend since kindergarten, Gary Claborn, provided photographs that he took at reunions of the old team. His pictures remind us how much time has passed since those guys piled up 36 victories in 37 games. Pat Thomas Brannon exhibited her love of Sylvan High and even did some copyediting. Norma McLendon, the advisor of *The Bear Facts*, shared years of memories and when I sent her a copy of the manuscript she assured me she would not cover the pages with red marks. Old grads Herb Britt and Bobby Ward remembered the year Sylvan High opened and Earl Shell talked about seasons without a home court. My wife, the former Kaye Howell, understood when I was late for dinner and provided much needed editing.

Ozzie Wadewitz was unable to speak for himself but his daughter, Angie Chesin, and his brother Richard, helped tell his story. Richard Wadewitz's tales about growing up over the family meat market were particularly compelling.

This is an old story but I used new methods of reporting. Through Facebook, I reached generations of Sylvan people that I don't even know. Their comments online were invaluable.

Finally, there is Charlie Walker. As Chief of Maintenance, he is trying to keep our old school alive. He showed me parts of the building I had never seen before and reminded me that love for Sylvan did not end when it was no longer a high school.

An important voice could not be heard and like so many others I miss Virlyn Gaynes. For he, Lee DeFore, Tommy Roberts, Terry Stephens and Bob Tuggle will always be Ozzie's Boys.

RICHARD HYATT

About the Author

O zzie's Boys has bounced around in Richard Hyatt's head for decades. He is a 1962 graduate of Sylvan High School so this is a story he understands very well.

Hyatt has been an award-winning reporter and columnist for newspapers in Georgia for more than 40 years. Most of his career was spent with the *Ledger-Enquirer* in Columbus where he provided generations of readers a look at events of the day and the fascinating stories behind them. His work also appears on www.richardhyattcolumbus.com — his news and opinion Website.

The author of 14 books, he has earned scores of state and regional journalism awards, including the prestigious Green Eyeshade Award. *Georgia Trend* named him one of the state's most influential journalists.

A native of Atlanta, he attended Georgia State University and graduated from Columbus State University. Hyatt lives in Columbus with his wife Kaye and their daughter Kamryn. He has two other daughters, Heather and Kaitlin.

Books by Richard Hyatt

The Carters of Plains

Those Trees Are Mine

Lewis, Jack & Me

Kermit: Like the Frog

Buick Southern Open: The First 25 Years

Nothin' But Fine: The Music and the Gospel According to Jake Hess

Zell: The Governor Who Brought HOPE to Georgia

Mr. Speaker: A Biography of Tom Murphy

Charles Jones: A Biography

Home of the Infantry: A History of Fort Benning

Reflections on a Legacy: A History of the Country Club of Columbus

From These Hills: A History of Green Island Country Club

Richard Hyatt's Columbus: Remembering 40 Years of Daily Journalism

Ozzie's Boys: The Story of Sylvan High School

Made in the USA
Charleston, SC
18 January 2012